BORN ENOUGH

The Holistic Blueprint to Remembering

ONDREA LYNN

ISBN: 978-1-0918-0972-7

Disclaimer

The information provided in this book is designed to provide helpful information on the subjects discussed. This book is not meant to be used, nor should it be used, to diagnose or treat any medical condition. For diagnosis or treatment of any medical problem, consult your own physician. The publisher and author are not responsible for any specific health or allergy needs that may require medical supervision and are not liable for any damages or negative consequences from any treatment, action, application or preparation, to any person reading or following the information in this book. The reader should regularly consult a physician in matters relating to his/her health and wellness. References are provided for informational purposes only and do not constitute endorsement of any websites or other sources.

I dedicate this book to you,

Wanda Marilyn Mead, my grandma.

You would have gone to jail or died in a fight for any one of us. Yes, I remember when you told me this! I wish you could really feel that love for yourself that I have for you.

CONTENTS

Foreword

Jennifer Urezzio, Founder, Soul Language

FOR MANY OF US, the "not enough" journey begins long before birth and generally appears to be a consistent aspect of the human condition. Often, the road back to remembering that we are whole and complete requires tools, practices, consciousness, and love.

I have an intimate knowledge of the journey to enoughness, and I'm so grateful that there are now more tools than ever before—including this book—to support people's growth.

The personal stories and case studies in Ondrea's book support the reader in knowing they are not alone and there is a pathway to remembering and experiencing their innate wholeness.

This is truly an ongoing process. The big theme of "not enough" will continue to come up in a person's life—especially when they are desiring more love, abundance and Divinity within their lives and consciousness.

This book in itself is a testament to Ondrea's determination to move from "not enough" to completeness. I recommend that readers of the book recall Ondrea's resolve when they struggle with their own enoughness.

One of the chapters I am most excited about is "Eating to Enough." The idea of eating to support completeness is a concept I believe many people are unfamiliar with, and if they follow the process in this chapter alone, it may change their experience forever.

I have dedicated my life to helping people understand their soul and become more conscious, and this topic of enoughness is one that arises time and time again. A sacred space is required that individuals can access regularly to remind themselves of the truth that they are enough, whole, and complete. I believe this book can help readers create that place.

Our journeys and our movement through them are individual and very personal, and the questions for inner-guidance in this book support an easier expedition of discovery.

A Note from the Author

I GUESS YOU WOULD call me a farm girl from New York. My great-grandparents owned an apple farm, and I spent a lot of time as a young girl playing in the orchards with my cousin. Life there was fun and free.

That's where my story really starts, on that farm and with my grandmother, Wanda Marilyn Mead.

My journey has led me to believe, if you transform your energy, it impacts all those who have come before you and all those who come after you. This belief brings me deep comfort.

My grandmother grew up on an apple farm in New York. On the farm, she worked many hours, which led her to sacrifice her childhood and her education.

She had an overprotective mother. The result was a life of restrictions; few friends and no social life. I adored my grandmother, and it saddened me to hear her stories about wanting to get out of her parent's house so badly, that she married a man she knew wasn't right for her.

Personally, I felt the best thing that happened was she found out he was cheating on her. This led her to make the decision to end the marriage. I was there the day this came to light and witnessed the profound impact this news had on her. It was the only day I saw my grandmother cry.

Even though the experience upset her, I believe it ended her future suffering in that partnership. I observed how his infidelity became her problem, because she believed she wasn't good enough and questioned what she did wrong.

My grandmother was my rock. Since my mom worked nights, I spent most of my time at her house. I even had my own room there. She was my defender. She showed her fist to the girls who were mean to me and showed her shotgun to the mean boys.

I was dating a boy who would often park in the apple orchard across from the house. He was loud and disrespectful, and at night, he would park his car in the orchard and spy on me. My grandma finally had had enough of the harassment, and one night, she went outside with her shotgun and hid, waiting for him.

When he drove up, she shot a bullet at his windshield as a warning. He never came back. At the time, it was embarrassing, but now I can laugh about it. The thought of my friends finding out about that episode was mortifying. I would have been the girl with the crazy grandmother, and no one would have wanted to hang out with me.

As you can tell, she wasn't your typical cuddly granny. She made sure I had hot homemade meals daily, but how she really showed her love for me by being tough and strict, which always made me feel safe.

As long as I can remember, my grandmother struggled with loving herself. The harshness extended to herself and showed up in how she didn't care for herself.

My grandparents owned horses and participated in shows. One day, an argument arose with my grandfather about the horse trailer. She was so angry that she decided to try and lift the 2,000-pound trailer herself, and she injured her back severely.

To me, this is a clear example of her toughness spilling over into not caring for herself. She never really recovered from that injury; despite many surgeries, she still experienced back pain. She would talk about herself in negative ways by saying she was not smart or pretty enough. She always was presentable, and I would look in her closet and see the beautiful dresses and wonder why she wasn't wearing them. She seemed like she wanted to keep herself hidden from the world. She never liked her body and was always wishing it to be different.

Recently, she was looking at a picture of herself from a few years ago, and she commented, "If I only could look like that picture again." I said to her, "When you took that picture, you didn't like the way you looked, either. When will you look in the mirror and love what you see, Grandma?" She began to get teary-eyed, and I let her know I loved her and the subject of her worthiness wasn't closed.

In that moment, I thought two things:

- I wish she could see the depths of her beautiful soul, the way I can see it.
- I must make a change in my own life, so, when I am her age, I can feel and know my soul's worth.

Her lack of self-worth led her to choose jobs that were physically demanding, because she never thought she was smart enough to branch out into anything different.

Her heart was a generous one, and her doors were always open to friends and family who might need a place to stay until they could get on their feet again. I believe, if she'd felt better about herself, those doors would have shut on those whom she knew were taking advantage of her.

I don't know what will happen to how my grandmother feels and views herself. I do know that observing her, and her love for me, taught me I could not continue the path of unworthiness. I believed I had to transform my own unworthiness because of what I witnessed with my grandmother. She is very brave to continue to fight to be enough, but that is a very long and tiresome way to transform. What I realized is you can make a different choice, and if she decided to choose differently, it could change everything for her. She could choose to believe that she is enough and to feel that in every situation.

I have unchained and broken many aspects of the not-enough cycle. I will continue to do so for my family and myself, so we can be free. By choosing to truly love myself, I will make choices that reflect that love. I know that loving myself more will impact my children and my descendants.

I want my grandmother to know the truth of who she is: amazing, strong, smart, beautiful, talented, creative, and someone who can fix anything. I would love it if she could feel the truth of who she is, which is a radiant soul who comes from God, beautiful, loving, and full of light. I would also love it if she could remember she is a part of the infinite creation that is perfectly perfect.

I see and feel the love she has for her family, and I know she only wants the best for us. In these pages, you are going to read about how believing you are unworthy impacts your world; also, about my journey and others' to enoughness. You will also have the opportunity to utilize my tools and the exercises I developed to create the belief in worthiness. The road might be a little rocky at times, but I assure you it is worth it.

This book is filled with tangible examples of how feeling not enough shows up in our lives. I highly suggest you make notes in a journal or in the margins of these pages about what resonates with you, as you read these stories. The biggest part of healing unworthiness is first coming to the conclusion that you are enough. And that takes self-discovery.

Chapter 1

Trying to Show the World I'm Good:

My Family History and Story of Not Enoughness

MY GRANDMOTHER'S APPLE farm was, for me, a safe haven. My cousin and I had a special rock out back that we called Big Rock. That is where we would have deep conversations and share our secrets.

My parents divorced when I was only two, so it was my regular topic of conversation on the Big Rock. I remember so vividly their arguments and fights; Mom screaming as Dad just screamed back, neither one of them making any sense. The Big Rock was the only place I felt I could be me and experience a deep sense of peace.

They both remarried. My mother had two more marriages, and my father married a woman who resembled the wicked stepmother in *Cinderella*. She was emotional and mentally abusive to me when my father wasn't around. As soon as my father walked through the door, her manner changed completely.

As I got older, we didn't spend much time at the farm. Life was busy, with school, dance and singing classes, and social events. I found a new way and a new element to share my heartfelt feelings and worries. I shared my thoughts with the trees.

At my mother's house, we had a back porch, and I would go out there and talk to the trees and then dance for them, so I could feel better. It always made a world of a difference.

My world changed when I was eleven, after I was sexually assaulted by a family member. I was too young to understand what was happening. The abuse escalated over time, starting with "minor" actions, like sleeping near me. I was confused and didn't truly understand what was happening. I would wake up with his hand on my private parts. I longed for the Big Rock; my time with the trees wasn't producing the same impact of peace and enoughness.

The only person I told was a close friend. Eventually, her conscience could not keep it a secret anymore, and she told her mother. Of course, guess what? My friend's mother told my mother. After my mother found out, what little peace I'd had in my life seemed to evaporate.

Each member of my family acted differently. My mother didn't look at or talk to me. Life went on in my family, and no one seemed to address the situation except my father, who badgered me about the abuse. There was this elephant in the room that no one would admit was there.

My eleven-year-old self felt like I had done something wrong. I thought, when my family looked at me, all they could think about was how terrible I was. I felt marked. The worst part, more damaging than the abuse, was that my biological father didn't believe me. He kept asking me if I was making this up to gain attention. My father was in denial.

My mother was depressed. She struggled with depression all her life, and the situation of my abuse seemed to have exacerbated it. I was alone.

In an attempt to understand the situation, my stepfather wanted to know all the details of the experience. All I wanted to do was crawl in a hole and hide forever.

This series of events created a rage inside of me that I didn't know how to express. I began to focus my anger on my dream of becoming a famous performer. Over and over again, I said to myself, "I'll show the world I'm good."

The rage and hate for my abuser and the those who denied my abuse grew inside of me. From that moment forward, with everything I did and every choice I made, I was going to prove to them that I was better than they were.

I know now that what I was really trying to do was prove to my family I was good enough. For me, fame and fortune were equivalent to being good enough and being loved.

My love of dance started at the age of five, and it became a safe haven for me. My life seemed to be full of disappointments and struggles, unless I was dancing.

Still pursuing my dream of being a performer and proving my enoughness, at seventeen, I auditioned for Julliard. Once again, I felt out of place in that room. I was surrounded by tall, thin girls. I was forced to the back of the room in order not to be trampled by the other girls, when we began to dance. I felt lost and as if I didn't exist. The audition was a disaster.

I left that audition and thought thank God, that was over and I was free. I dusted myself off and asked now what? That question led me to apply to the American Musical and Dramatic Academy (AMDA) in Manhattan. I was accepted.

The school was amazing for me, because it allowed me to lose myself in dance and music and find a place where I felt at home. I hadn't felt that way since sitting on the Big Rock or chatting with the trees.

During my time there, I kept hearing from my instructors that I would be an amazing performer and have the hearts of the audience if:

- I let down my walls.
- I could allow myself to truly be free when I dance.

All this advice, which I know now to be true, I only heard then as my not being enough.

As I danced, I would critique my movements, and this overthinking kept me out of the flow of the dance. I couldn't allow the truth that I was enough to be displayed in my dancing. It seemed I was always stuck in analysis. I was surrounded by other amazing dancers and would look at their greatness but could never see that within myself. All I was able to see was my weakness.

Deep inside me, I knew there was a light and truth, and I was determined to find and experience it. I set out to understand how to unleash all the goodness inside of me.

I Am Not Alone

Does this part of my story sound familiar to you? Ever just feel incomplete? You have just read about my experience and feelings. It is challenging to put into words this feeling of incompleteness, because we may be too close to it and it can impact so many areas of our lives.

Since this pattern of feeling incomplete and not enough is so embedded in our lives, you might not be fully aware of all the experiences you are creating based on this pattern.

My experiences of not enoughness resulted in me, as a teenager, hanging around older kids who were drinking and using marijuana. I felt as if there was a huge hole in me, as if there was a part missing, which led me to choose to join in the partying. I was under the impression that making this choice would fill the hole inside. It didn't.

This feeling that a piece was missing also created in me a distorted relationship with my body. I took every opportunity to beat up my body, from starving myself to binge eating to taking laxatives. My relationship with my body went way beyond just wishing my thighs were thinner and my breasts were bigger. I would often run around the house to lose weight, until my body just gave out.

Even though I had a lot of friends in school, I never really felt as though I was part of anything. In school, I felt like an outcast, even though I acted as if I was totally comfortable. I spent a lot of my waking hours wishing and wanting to look and act like my friends. In fact, at times, I would try to model how they talked and walked, desperately trying to fit in in order to fill that hole inside of me.

I hid my true self because I was ashamed of these dark feelings inside of me. To ensure I was safe, I would pick fights, be bossy, and project a "mean girl" attitude.

We have all had life experiences (as children and adults) that have been painful and created feelings of shame, not enough, or incompleteness. When you are experiencing the "not enough" syndrome, these experiences are overwhelming. If no one has told you yet, I will: *you are not alone.*

There are a few experiences that stand out for me that added to the "not enough" hole that was growing inside of me. This overwhelming feeling of not enough was exacerbated by my being a child of divorce, by my mom's struggles with depression, and by my being sexually assaulted by a family member at age eleven.

I was an individual who felt there was a hole inside me, and I had enough experience to prove to myself that I was not good enough to fill the emptiness, so I abused my physical, mental, and spiritual bodies in many ways.

The only weight problem I had was in my head. I wanted to be thinner, so I would put myself on a Sunday fast, not eating anything and drinking only water until 5 p.m. Or I would break down and binge eat everything and anything I could find in my house. I would take pills, such as laxatives.

If abusing my physical body with food wasn't bad enough, I began to drink and use drugs with friends and have sex, because I was hoping it would make me feel better about myself. Guess what? It always made me feel worse.

All of the above choices just added to my confusion around feeling not enough. The thoughts in my head led me to choices that were directly the opposite of what I wanted and were abusive to me. When I made a choice that I knew wasn't in my best interest, I would unleash the nasty girl in my head and berate myself.

My soul... Well, I was ignoring it totally, and when I would sit in meditation (because I started meditating at the age of seventeen), I felt fear. So much fear would come up, it was like the boogie man in the closet!

I reached out for guidance and support by praying and pulling angel cards. All the support and guidance were the same: *you need to love yourself, open your heart more, and feel safe*. The guidance was all about me, but all I wanted to hear was tangible information, like when would I meet the love of my life. I would keep pulling card after card and receive the same messages. I would then insist to my soul and my spirit guides that the guidance I was getting wasn't good enough.

Reflecting back now, knowing what I know, I can see how not enough was ruling my life and decisions.

What I have seen in many of the women with whom I have worked with over the years, is they are totally numbed to their past. They tell me those times are over and it was a long ago. Little do people understand how much your history impacts you, unless you address it. When you don't address pain, it becomes suffering. Suffering is when you keep ignoring things, stuffing your feelings, and pretending that history doesn't exist. I'm not saying you won't feel the pain again; I'm saying that you are creating a lot of unnecessary suffering by not looking pain in the eye.

You Are Not Alone

Mary came in to see me for a session. She struggled with weight. She was doing all the right things with food, but the scale was not budging. Her digestion was off, and her joints often felt achy.

Her not enoughness was not only showing up in her body, it was reflected back to her with her struggles with money and love relationships. She had a past with emotional and mental abuse from a family member.

During her hour-long session, she shared many memories of her past. Her mother was an alcoholic and had a temper. Her older brother bore the brunt of the mother's physical abuse, so he, in turn, physically abused Mary.

As I listened and intuitively tuned in, I saw these memories stuck in her physical body. This past pain was creating a feeling of tightness in her lower back and a pattern of being stuck in a rut.

She had created energetic walls to protect herself from experiencing pain again. This created distance between her and the world and was not at the frequency to attract men.

Mary was sending out an energy of being shut down. We conducted some energy work. During our time together, I noticed that her second and third chakras were very restricted. By my setting the intention that Divine love supported that area, there was an increase of light and flow. Then, we cut the energetic cords connecting her to her mother and brother. Those cords were draining her energy and flow. After cutting the cords, she seemed to come back into balance.

I then asked her higher self and her body what movement would help support her in liberating these energies, and we did the exercises together.

Your higher self is the highest aspect of the real and complete you. It is the part that is in union with a supreme/Divine consciousness.

The movement I suggested for Mary is a strength and confidence-building exercise called the *Vitality Exercise*. I shared with her the foods her body needed to support the new energy and soul expansion. (This process is described in detail in the exercise section of the book. I also list the foods I shared with her in that portion of the book.)

Some of the specific foods that coincided with her vitality exercise were orange and yellow peppers, carrots, and yellow squash. These would specifically strengthen and expand her second and third chakra (see basic chakra system in the resource section later in the book) centers, which are housed in this area of her body.

After our time together, she felt renewed and a deep sense of clarity about who she was and what her next steps would be.

Two days after our session, she began to spiral out of control with food. Nothing she ate satisfied her and she couldn't get enough food. When she called me, consumed with worry and fear, I asked, "What are you feeding? There is an emptiness inside you that you are trying to fill with food, and you will never do it. What holes are you still trying to fill with food, alcohol, drugs, sex, etc.?"

When I asked her these questions, she expressed feeling a life-changing awareness, and she started to understand her pattern in a new way.

She was going to take a few days and journal her feelings. She was beginning to create a bridge to move from the beliefs of being unworthy that were generating most of her "bad" feelings, to those of worthiness and love. Mary had new tools to create long-lasting transformation.

You will hear more about Mary later, when we discuss some of the results of being enough.

Your Awareness

You've read about Mary's and my not enoughness experiences and stories. What's your story of not enoughness? How does it show up in your life? How do you try and fill the hole inside of you?

As we end this first chapter, I want to provide you with some exercises that can help fill the void you have been noticing. Since, there are different parts of us—mind, body, and spirit—the exercise *Filling the Imaginary Void* addresses each aspect (mind, body, spirit) individually.

Unworthiness brings a feeling of emptiness, and it will show up differently for everyone. These exercises will help you explore how you are filling that imaginary void in an unsustainable way.

When you are aware of how you are filling this void, you can begin to make conscious choices to fill it with love, power, and worthiness.

Exercise for Transformation: Filling the Imaginary Void

❖ The Element of the Mind

Grab a pen and paper/journal. Make a list of all the ways you feel at this time, where you are filling the void. Some examples are

- ✓ overeating
- ✓ undereating
- ✓ binge eating
- ✓ diet pills
- ✓ starving yourself
- ✓ doing activities to stay busy
- ✓ over-obsessing
- ✓ not taking care of your bills
- ✓ buying items you don't need
- ✓ avoiding your to-do list
- ✓ oversleeping
- ✓ over-exercising
- ✓ not exercising at all
- ✓ eating a lot of sugary sweets and carbs.

It's "normal" if you have a long list. It's important that you don't judge yourself during this or any exercise.

Circle the top three things you notice you do daily or weekly.

Once you have your top three, now put a star at the one you do most often. Ask yourself are you really ready to make this shift? If yes, move forward with the exercise. If no, then take a day and sit with everything you have written on this page. Ask yourself how are those patterns serving you?

Once you realize and truly feel that the list of actions is no longer serving you in the way you need it to, you can then say YES to making the shift.

The Shift: Look at your number-one pattern (the one you placed a star next to). Ask yourself, when you are in this pattern, what different choice could you make?

Then write out a list of some potential new actions.

For the next few days, every time you notice you are participating in your number-one pattern (the starred item) , consider it an opportunity to choose to do one of the potential new actions from the list you made.

Over time, this will create a new pathway in your brain that will make this literally a no-brainer. You will just begin to make the new choice without even thinking about it.

❖ The Element of the Body

Your core is in the center of your body, located from your upper abdominal area to your hip area. (This includes the front and back of your body.)

Studies show, if the core is strong, you are less likely to have issues in other areas of your body. It is your powerhouse, as you need this part of your body for everything you do, including sitting in a chair. This part of you also houses your second and third chakras, which are about action and creativity, feelings and personal power, respectively.

Many years ago, I studied with a shaman who taught me that our soul's truth sits right above the belly button area. Now you can see why the core is very important, as it houses your truth and power. I feel it is vital to work your core when you are feeling a void.

There is one exercise that is great at helping the body to remember its truth and power while building its strength. It is called a *plank*.

Here is how to begin if this is something new for you.

- Start on your hands and knees.
- Stay on your knees, pull your belly in toward your spine, and drop onto your forearms, sliding your forearms out until your hips drop down, as if your upper body was like a tabletop.
- Hold 15-30 seconds. Rest for a minute and repeat 2 more times.

If you have done plank but don't do them on a regular basis:

- Start on your forearms and knees; pull your belly in towards your spine.
- Tuck your toes under and lift your knees off the floor while dropping your hips down forming a table top with your body. Hold 30-40 seconds.
- Rest for a minute and repeat 2 more times.

If you are an avid planker and your body needs a little challenge:

- Start on your forearms and knees; pull your belly in towards your spine.
- Tuck your toes under and lift your knees off the floor while dropping your hips down forming a table top with your body.
- Lift your right leg up slightly off the ground and hold for 30 seconds then lift the left leg up and hold for 30 seconds.
- Then rest for a minute and repeat 2 more times.

During this exercise, no matter if you are a beginner or advanced, you may experience this feeling of not being able to do it. Your physical body may not be able to hold for the full time. It is okay. Be gentle with yourself and keep trying daily. You will notice you will begin to hold a little longer, as long as you keep at it.

Every part of you may tremble. Remember: you are building strength in your truth and personal power center. As long as there is no pain, be persistent.

❖ The Element of the Spirit

When you feel disconnected from your Higher Self, you feel empty. When you feel disconnected from God/Creator, you feel an array of things, specifically feeling lost and worthlessness.

Your Higher Self is the highest aspect of you that you can attain and hold, while in physical existence. When you feel the presence of your Higher Self and Creator, you will no longer feel the deep void or want to fill it with unhealthy thoughts, foods, sexual acts, and material items.

You will be using the mantra or affirmation, *I AM that I AM.* This is a holy mantra that expresses the agreement between you and God, according to *The Book of Enoch*.

- Begin by finding a quiet place and a comfortable seat
- Say to yourself three times, "I AM that I AM"
- Take three deep breaths, and notice your thoughts. During the deep breaths, allow your thoughts to float away.
- Tune into your heart, and sense love there. What color is in your heart? What do you sense, feel, or experience?

- Hold that color in your heart while saying again, "I AM that I AM." Allow this color to expand in any other part of your body or energy field.
- Allow the color to expand in those places where you feel the void, or set the intention that the color will fill the void.
- Notice how this color or colors begins to pulsate around you as you fill the void.
- Notice you are surrounded by the most sparkling golden light. This is the golden light of God/Creator/Love surrounding you and all the colors that have expanded from your heart. The golden light begins to mix with your colors. Sit with this for a few moments, as your higher self and God/Creator/Love integrate more with your physical body. Take a breath and just allow.
- When you feel this is complete, take a nice deep breath and open your eyes, coming back to be present and centered in your body.

In this, you may experience a feeling of floating, your heart opening, which will bring a flood of emotions up and out. Or you may feel nothing. Just know that something is happening, no matter what the experience.

The most important part is you will feel lighter and your mood lifted, the more you conduct this exercise. Doing this daily for at least thirty days will make a big difference in how connected you feel to your higher self and God/Creator/Love. In doing the above exercises, you will fill the void and release those feelings of emptiness.

Chapter 2

Why? Why Do I Feel So Empty?

THAT IS THE ULTIMATE question, isn't it?

I would love to give you a quick answer and say this is the reason why, but *you* are complex. To identify why not enough is holding your life hostage, I will explain not enough behavior and expressions.

Just as every person is very different and unique, so is the expression of "not enough". It doesn't discriminate; it's not based on race, ethnicity, color, sex, gender, religion, or age. Though it may show itself differently, the root of it is a feeling of a profound sense of unworthiness, which leads to disconnection and lack of self-love that expresses itself in examples of not enough behavior.

The feelings of not enough are like an adaptive virus. It is a call to be aware and turn toward a bigger truth. To be ahead of the virus, you must be aware and keep utilizing transformational tools.

What does not enough look like/feel like and why does it happen?

Here are some general examples of how "not enough" shows up in life and how it feels:

You might consider making some notes in a journal or in the margin, if you feel these examples are how your own not enough expresses itself.

- You Agree with People, Even When It Doesn't Feel in Alignment with Your Own Beliefs

Carol is at a gathering to celebrate women in business. She is seated at a table with eleven other women, who begin to discuss parenting and how wonderful it is. As they rave about their children, she feels this pressure to smile and go along with the conversation.

Carol feels, by nodding, she isn't being true to herself. For Carol, even though she has moments of happiness and connection, her experience of parenting is that it is a tough job. She feels like the core of being a parent is tough love, sleepless nights, and a heavy heart. Carol's not enoughness is being triggered, and she is too shy to share of her feelings and experiences.

- ❖ You Look for Compliments, especially from the Opposite Sex, Looking to Men to Make You Feel Wanted and Validated

Amanda gets all dressed up to have a long overdue night out at a bar with her closest girlfriends. She spends the whole time there trying to catch the eye of every man in the place and gain their attention. Each of her friends tells her she looks amazing, but it feels like not enough until she hears it from a man. By the end of the night, she has not attracted the attention of any man, and she goes home feeling unwanted and incomplete.

- ❖ You Date Individuals Who Mentally Abuse You

Kathryn was dating Dan for several months. As the relationship progressed, after they were intimate, Dan would make comments like, "You would be stunning if your breasts were bigger or stomach were flatter." These comments made her feel awful, but her not enough prevented her from telling him to stop making those comments.

- ❖ You Use Sex to Feel Enough

Sara was married to Ken, who owned a restaurant. Sara helped out by waitressing. During her shift, Ken would berate Sara by asking her if there was something wrong with her brain, grab the ticket or pen out of her hand while she was taking a customer's order, and do it himself because he felt she wasn't fast enough.

Ken sang a different tune after the shift, when they were at home. He would tell her how attractive she was, and they would make love. Sara would have a moment of feeling good about herself. And then, the next day, the process would start all over-again.

- ❖ You Hold Yourself Back

Carmine was working as a personal trainer in a local gym for a few years. When she began her business, she worked as many hours as she could, to grow her clientele. After having a baby, she had cut back to twenty work hours a week.

Every month, the gym ran a report of sales and gave bonuses to their employees who hit specific sales goals. Carmine was always first or second in line to receive a bonus, even while working only twenty hours a week.

The position for the director of personal training was about to open up, and she knew, if she applied and was accepted, this would help her family thrive financially. When it was time to apply, though, she began to have thoughts and doubts: Could she really do this position? What if her peers didn't like her because she was the boss? And what if she didn't know something?

Carmine got lost in the fear instead of taking action, and the result was she held herself back and someone else applied and received the position.

❖ You Constantly Compare Your Body to Others

One day, Nancy's ten-year-old daughter was invited over to a friend's house. When Nancy dropped her daughter off, she saw a big, beautiful house with the most perfect landscaped lawn. Nancy walked her daughter to the door, and a tall, very slim, and fit woman decked in Lululemon clothing greeted her.

As Nancy returned to her car, she was comparing her home and clothes to her daughter's friend's mother. A wave of depression hit her. After seeing the fit mom, her hate for her slight belly and thicker thighs burned inside of her.

❖ You Stay Quiet in Situations Because You Are Afraid of Rejection

Mary Lou worked in a corporate position. There was a misunderstanding between two of her co-workers about a specific project. As they got into a heated debate, she began to become more and more reserved, even though she had valuable input toward a resolution.

She was unable to voice her opinion because she believed she wasn't worthy of expressing her truth and would be rejected.

- You Hide Your Body

Jane was a gymnast most of her early childhood years. Because of this, her thighs were a little more stocky and muscular than other women's. Now that she was in her forties, her body had changed a bit, but her legs were still holding their tone rather well.

She refused to wear jeans or leggings, however, so she didn't have to show her legs. She chose to wear baggy sweatpants or long skirts, instead. Jane didn't want attention brought to her toned legs, because she thought they were ugly, even though any woman in her forties would envy them.

- You Feel Like You Want to Hide in Groups

Tabatha had a group of friends she had known for over ten years. They got together every Friday evening to catch up, either at a local restaurant or one of their houses.

No matter where they met up, Tabatha acted shy and a little standoffish. Her friends often asked her if she was okay, and she answered yes, even though she never felt comfortable in anyone's presence. She usually found herself sitting with the same person every time and not freely walking around, connecting deeply with all the others.

If you'd asked her to articulate this, she wouldn't have had the words. She didn't want to talk about her life because, in her eyes, it didn't look as exciting as her friends'.

- You Put Others on a Pedestal

Caroline was always attracted to angels, growing up. Every time she went shopping with her mom, she begged for a statue of an angel. She wanted to fill her room with statues of angels. She had this attraction to them because she felt their presence often, and, as she got older, she began to see them in her mind's eye during meditation.

In her early twenties, Caroline took classes to learn more about the topic of angels. The teacher, who was about fifteen years older than she, had affiliations with angels and shared many inspiring stories of how they helped her, personally and professionally. Caroline experienced some hero worship with her teacher, and that led to her doubting her own connection and experiences.

During this time, her experiences with the angels became more frequent, and she felt their support and guidance. She began to share that guidance with her friends and family. In pure excitement, she started to share this with her teacher, too, who listened and then expressed that Caroline's experiences were not real.

She disregarded her sharing. Caroline went into quiet mode and stopped sharing, as she felt the teacher knew best.

- You Self-Sabotage

Alice was an aspiring actress. She spent hours a day sending out resumés and looking for casting calls that would be right for her. As exhausting as it felt at times, she continued to plug away, although for months there was a professional drought, without any call-backs.

One day, she received a message from a casting director, but instead of calling back instantly, she delayed a day.

- You Judge Others

Mae was a quiet woman who lived in a small town. She had a good job, a beautiful home, and healthy children. Every time she met someone in public, she greeted them with a big smile, but then, as they walked away from her, she would comment negatively on their appearance or their character.

- You Gossip

Claire thrives on getting the scoop about other people's lives. The more gossip she hears, especially if it involves hearing how other people are struggling, the better she feels about her life. It makes her uncomfortable to share about herself, so she chooses to talk about others, in order to keep the uncomfortable feelings at bay.

- You Try to Control People and/or Situations

Claire also thinks she knows what is best for others. When she went camping with friends, she told each of them what the group was going to do and when they were going to do it. This did not allow for fun, because, if things did not go her way, she got very flustered and either started an argument or cried.

- You Force Your Views or Beliefs on Others

Melissa was introduced to healthy eating in her early thirties. She watched every documentary she could find on clean eating. Melissa then made drastic changes in her life by cutting out processed sugars and meat.

About a year later, she took a big jump and became vegan. During her journey, she shared very openly with her family and on social media about what she was learning and why she'd made the decision to transform her health.

She began to share pictures of animals being slaughtered on social media, saying things like, "If you didn't make this shift to being vegan, you are the reason innocent animals die." She would sit next to her sister during family gatherings and pick apart every bad ingredient and how each impacts the body. Melissa would often judge people or try to force her view on them, making it very challenging to be around her.

- You Have Trouble Listening and Feel the Need to Talk Incessantly

Louise loves to be around people. She participates in a handful of social organizations that meet weekly. When she attends meetings, she tends to monopolize the conversation. When someone tries to interject, she may pause for a second, but then she continues on with her current story about herself.

- You Struggle with Money

Samantha had owned a health club for about two years. She bought it knowing the wellness industry was rapidly growing in her area. The club was making monthly goals, but Samantha wasn't happy with the income level. Her goal was to double the current monthly income. It seemed, though no matter what she did as advertising, nothing changed.

Most people thought she must be well-off financially, owning her own business, but she was just getting by and worried about her future and savings.

- You Put Your Focus on the Physical

Amber was a forty-two-year-old shopaholic. Her main priority every week was to get her mani-pedi, facial, and a new dress for Friday night dinner with her husband.

This was her third marriage and Amber's husband was Prince Charming. He adored her and gave her whatever she wanted. Like in her other marriages, Amber couldn't seem to be present in the marriage. Her husband truly wanted her to be happy, but Amber didn't understand that *thinking* you are happy and *being* happy were two different things. Everything she did was for external reasons, in order to look a certain way to the world. She couldn't figure out why, if she looked great, why she didn't feel great.

While Amber was growing up, her mother abandoned the family, which left her father to raise her and her sister. As soon as she was old enough to live on her own, she put all her attention on how aesthetically she presented herself to the world. She worked out and got her hair and nails done weekly, but never took the time to explore herself deeper. She had not looked at her feelings or how she could experience more joy in her marriage.

❖ You Have to Keep Up with the Joneses

Tina, who was in her early thirties, admired nice things. She created a home that was beautiful and expertly decorated, but she still wouldn't invite people over, because she felt shame that her home was not furnished with top-name brands.

❖ You Ignore Your Body

Stephanie experienced a low-back issue for over five years. The doctors couldn't determine anything wrong with her, yet she still felt discomfort daily. She was guided to drink more water to help hydrate her body, which will loosen up the muscles, but she never made it a priority. Her nurse practitioner also suggested she begin a daily, three-minute stretching routine. But after months, she still had not incorporated that into her life.

- You Choose Relationships in Which You are Undervalued

Wanda has a long-time friend from high school named Judy. After twenty years, they were still close, yet Wanda was starting to feel this friendship was one-sided. Judy didn't own a car, and she constantly called Wanda to pick her up and take her shopping. Wanda always answered Judy's call. Judy never thanked Wanda or offered gas money or said yes, when Wanda herself asked for support.

- You Choose Relationships Where You are Bullied

Zariah was getting married, and her cousin, who was also her best friend, was the maid of honor. She was so excited and wanted her closest friend to be a part of every decision. During the planning of the wedding, they spent hours each day putting all the pieces together to create the special event.

At the final hour, there was an issue with the flower arrangements, and Zariah made a decision to change the entire arrangement. Her maid of honor was very upset with her decision, saying she should have been contacted because, with everything going on, Zariah couldn't make the best choice to benefit the entire wedding party.

- You Create Situations to Stand Out

In high school, Daisy struggled deeply with not enough. She would create situations in order to control how people were talking about her. She was so overwhelmed with feelings of not being part of the group that she made sure people were thinking she was unique and didn't want to be part of the rest of the class.

She would create daring outfits, and, if the entire class was going left, she would go right. She wasn't doing these things because they resonated with her; she was acting this way because she figured, if her classmates were going to reject her, then they were going to reject her on her own terms.

***

Some other signals that you believe you are not enough:

- **Pride:** there's never anything wrong, and you feel like you need to be perfect
- **Blame:** never taking responsibility for your role in your life
- **Compare:** spending time evaluating yourself to others and being resentful for others successes

- **Not enough:** not enough time, money, love, etc.
- **Deny:** lack of generosity with yourself, love, money, self-care, pleasure, etc.

Lack and Not Enough

The most obvious way that not enough shows up in our lives is feeling the lack of something. If you hear yourself repeating the not enoughs—not enough time, money, freedom, love, etc.— then it is safe to say you are experiencing a core belief of not enough.

What awarenesses are you having about how your own not enough shows up in your life? Are you beginning to see yourself in some of these not enough examples?

After reading through the examples and having some knowledge about how not enough shows up for you, are you starting to see how obvious the not enough is?

What is the cause of not being aware of these patterns and transforming them? Why do you need tools and support to break up with the not enough?

The answers: My personal opinion, from moving through it, is that when you are in the trenches of the not enough storm, it is challenging to see clearly. In my professional opinion, this begins at a young age, due to experiences with your immediate family, and so you don't know anything different. It is a learned behavior from one of your custodial role models growing up, which means you are mirroring what they have showed you. It has become deeply ingrained and feels so familiar, you need support to see it clearly and tools to create new habits.

I want to share with you some not-enough belief systems that were created because of family dynamics.

24K a Month to Crickets

Let me introduce you to Maureen. Maureen has a history of growing up with a mother who had a profound addiction problem. She shared with me stories of an unstable childhood and how she never felt safe, because they moved from apartment to apartment. Once, her family even lived on the street, because her mom used the money she'd made to feed her addiction, instead of paying the bills.

When Maureen was a teenager, she was able to work and have her own money. That created another challenge with her mom. Her mother would find her hidden money and use it for drugs. During Maureen's early twenties, her mother died from an overdose.

Maureen thought finally she was free to do what she longed for, which was to have a child of her own and provide that child with safety and comfort. She wanted to give her child all the things she'd wished for as a young girl. Little did Maureen understand she was trying to fill a hole of not-enoughness within her.

Not only did she have one child, but she had two. One of her children was diagnosed with autism, and this led her into a profession helping children with that challenge. By going against mainstream society and heading down uncharted roads in order to help her child, she was then guided into helping many other children and moms who were struggling with autism.

Maureen built a very successful business all by following the love in her heart for her child. Her monthly income was consistently $5,000. She also had been working on her self-love and worthiness, and the result was she felt safe to be present in her life and her business, so they became easier for her.

One month, through distributing a special offer, she opened the floodgates of her business, and the result was suddenly earning $24,000 per month.

This great success sparked old fears and patterns in Maureen. She noticed her dominant feeling was *I don't deserve this abundance* and *money makes you lonely.* This energy of feeling undeserving and worrying that money would be taken away or she couldn't perform to meet her clients' needs seeped into every new offer she made. After that, people were not signing up.

Always a Bridesmaid

Sally, who had been never been married, had a date with a man who seemed to check off all the boxes on her "ideal mate" list. Her list was based on witnessing her parents' unhealthy relationship and wanting something more.

Her parents met in high school and were married for many years. Her father was a hard-working man and never seemed present at home. He wasn't physically affectionate and was always too busy to join family outings or share a family dinner. Sally felt like he was moving through life like a zombie. She knew this was not the relationship she desired for her own life, yet she had seemed to attract the same type of man in past relationships.

Being faced with her possible dream mate brought up feelings of not good enough for Sally. The result was she went home and binge ate for days. This impacted how she felt about her body, her digestion, and her weight. Sally's pattern of not enough allowed the opportunity for love to slip away, because she didn't feel "good enough" to take the relationship further.

You will learn more about Maureen and Sally's transformations later on...

Chapter 3

Why Do You Feel Empty?

Your Family Stories

OUR PARENTS ARE the first people with whom we are in relationship. Our interactions with them are the basis of our future relationships. How they relate to their world is how we learn to relate to ours.

What are you aware of, reading Maureen's and Sally's stories? How do you feel the pattern of not enough formed for Maureen and Sally and showed up in their lives?

What experiences in your own childhood are creating chaos in your life?

I have developed several exercises to help you rewrite your history around the not enough and lack of self-worth that has formed because of parental relationships.

There are many depths to the feelings and beliefs of unworthiness. Those feelings could have formed simply from a comment or action by a parent. To move past this history, you must understand that your parents were operating on their own unworthy system. I will also touch upon this in a later chapter, "90 Days to Enoughness Plan," where I will talk in depth about forgiveness and not enough.

Now, you are no longer a child and you can make a choice about what you believe.

The next clearing exercises deal with feelings and emotions, so I want to take a moment first to explain the difference between emotions and feelings. Most of us use these words interchangeably and believe the meanings are the same, yet they are quite different.

Let's dive into emotions

Emotions take place in the amygdala, the area of the brain in charge of decision making, conscious thoughts, and reasoning. Emotions create bio-chemical and electrical reactions in the physical body that will alter your physical state.

The amygdala plays a role in emotional arousal, which is why you feel emotions so strongly and why they last longer. It's like an echo continuing to pulse throughout your system. Emotions are instinctive, which means they prompt the body for threats or rewards. You can witness the impact of emotions in the body by pupil dilation, pulse rate, facial expressions, and brain activity. Emotions are said to be hardwired in our DNA.

Here is an example of emotions at play. It is the holiday season, and Samantha is at a crowded mall, buying gifts for her two young boys. She gets bombarded by the people in the toy store, the lines are endless, and she is starving.

Across the store, she sees her best friend from high school, and before she can take a breath, she is overwhelmed with excitement. She rushes over to give her friend a huge hug, forgetting all about her earlier discomfort.

Let's dive into feelings

Unlike emotions, feelings take place in the neocortex of the brain. Feelings are colored by your personal life experiences, memories, and thoughts.

Here is an example to help you understand more of the difference between emotions and feelings. Katie was in a mentally abusive marriage for over ten years. Her divorce took several years, and there were a number of battles over the kids. Every time she saw an email come in from her husband, a wave of anxiety, dread, and worry came over her.

The most important point you need to remember is that emotions play out in the body and feelings play out in the mind.

As I have been immersed in writing about emotions versus feelings, I had some interesting things occur. I want to share these experiences with you, so you have some more tangible examples of how we are impacted by feelings and emotions.

I was asked to speak on a panel about postpartum depression after a new play called *Cal in Camo*. The play is about a raw welcome to motherhood. After the play ended, the panel began a deep discussion about the hidden plague of postpartum depression.

I had postpartum depression eighteen years ago, when my son was born. I was suffering with this depression without knowing it. The realization occurred when my son was six and I was explaining to someone how I was feeling and thinking. They said to me, "It sounds like you had postpartum depression."

I had never heard of postpartum depression, so I immediately conducted some research, and when I read the list of symptoms, I recognized my experience.

The panel organizer asked me to come up with three questions for the panel to discuss. A couple of days prior to the event, my body began speaking to me. My lower back became so tight and compressed. I stretched, did yoga, and walked to help loosen up the tension and still found no relief. This should have been the sign for me to ask what emotions were stuck in my body.

The night of the event, I took my spot on stage. I love being on stage, and any nerves I have usually vanish as soon as I am in the spotlight. As I began to share my story, though, my legs started to tremble.

What I didn't know when my son was born, but do know now, is that postpartum depression was instant for me. I was young when I had my son, and it was a very long, natural birth. When they handed my son to me, I said to my mother, "Whose baby is this?" She chuckled and said, "It is yours."

After this brief conversation with my mom, I remember my body began to tremble to the bone for many hours afterward. So, there I was, telling my story to an audience, and my body was doing the same thing, trembling to the bone.

As soon as the event ended, my legs stopped shaking. The very next morning, as I went to stand up, it was as if someone had stabbed me hard in my lower back. I fell back down to the seated position, wondering what just occurred.

My back went out so badly, I could barely walk and needed to see my chiropractor right away. It was the area of my back connected to feeling secure in your finances and in your career. Those two areas of my life took a direct hit when I got pregnant with my son.

I was an actress who did not have any other profession to fall back on, and my acting manager fired me after I gained seventy-five pounds. My back was holding these deep emotions for eighteen years, and finally it gave in. This experience forced me to look at those feelings and begin to release and regenerate myself.

I feel as though writing this and understanding emotions versus feelings has allowed me to move through that experience in a deeper way. Otherwise, I would have tossed it into the bag of being a little nervous and not put together the pieces for me to transition away from this trauma my body was holding.

Here is a quick reference guide from Laughter Online University:

Feelings	Emotions
Feelings tell us "**how to live**."	Emotions tell us what we "**like**" and "**dislike**."
Feelings state: "There is a **right and wrong** way to be."	Emotions state: "There are **good and bad** actions."
Feelings state: "**Your emotions matter.**"	Emotions state: "**The external world matters.**"
Feelings establish our **long-term attitude** toward reality.	Emotions establish our **initial attitude** toward reality.
Feelings alert us to **anticipated** dangers and prepares us for action.	Emotions alert us to **immediate** dangers and prepares us for action
Feelings ensure **long-term** survival of self. (body and mind.)	Emotions ensure **immediate** survival of self. (body and mind.)
Feelings are low-key but sustainable.	**Emotions are intense** but temporary.
Happiness is a feeling.	**Joy** is an emotion.
Worry is a feeling.	**Fear** is an emotion.
Contentment is a feeling.	**Enthusiasm** is an emotion.
Bitterness is a feeling.	**Anger** is an emotion.
Love is a feeling.	**Attraction** is an emotion.

Rewriting Parental History: Transformational Exercises

These exercises will bring conscious awareness to times that were suppressed or emotions and feelings that were not expressed. This experience allows for contemplation and reflection without being attached to these old moments/memories, by giving yourself permission to step back and witness.

Why is it important to release the not-enoughness around your family relationships? They were your first relationships and your models for love, safety, and enoughness.

You're going to be taking some notes, so please get pen and paper ready.

A great way to move into witness is by becoming an observer before you ask yourself the questions below. Here is a simple way to move into observer mode that works for me and many of my clients.

- First, begin by putting on your favorite song and dance around. This lifts your spirit and opens your heart.
- When your song is complete, take a seat, close your eyes, and imagine you are standing behind yourself. Imagine you are sitting in a movie theater watching yourself on the screen.

- Take a moment to remind yourself that you are safe and are able to see yourself much more clearly, now that you are no longer in the movie but watching it.
- Staying in this place, begin to look at the situations/scenarios listed below. This may be new for you so it is possible you have to keep coming back to this awareness until it becomes easier.

❖ The Mind

In the exercise below you will explore feelings and emotions. Don't hesitate to refer back to the chart to support you teasing out which are feelings versus emotions.

- List all the things your mother, father, or the people who had a major part in raising you said that activated the feelings of not good enough. (An example: You grew up with your mother always saying, "Children should be seen but never heard.")
- Now, list any actions those individuals might have taken that expressed not good enough. These actions could have been ones they made personally or actions they took toward you directly. Go with the first thoughts, feelings, and memories that come up, even if your conscious mind tries to tell you otherwise.

(An example: When you were a teenager and stayed out past your curfew, your father did not look at you or speak to you for weeks. It was as if you did not exist.)

- As you were making your list, did you notice how your mind chattered? Did your mind question the experience? Did you find yourself focusing on the disclaimer—"but they were good parents?"

  (An example: Well, I was a child who did not have the wisdom to speak. Or I was a silly teenager who deserved to be in trouble for breaking curfew.)

- What emotions did you experience? (An example: When you really think back on the moments when you heard, "Children should be seen but never heard," you feel this tightening in your upper chest and throat area. The emotion sitting in the body is that it is "a bad action" to speak.)

- Do any of those emotions reside in a location of your body? If so, where? If you don't "sense" it in your body, if you could place that emotion in your body, where would it be? (An example: Yes, as stated above, in my upper chest and throat area.)

- How many different emotions were you aware of while you were making your list?

- Now, offer yourself thanks. Thank your emotions, your body, and thank yourself for setting up these patterns to protect yourself.

  (An example: I have set up the pattern of not speaking up, and I can now thank it for how it has served me all these years. This will allow forgiveness and healing to occur. Awareness is also a big factor in breaking patterns you feel no longer serve you.)

Over the next few days, you might notice that emotions and feelings are still surfacing because of this exercise. If so, keep journaling what you notice. Be aware of your feelings, any discomfort in your body, and just offer those experiences gratitude.

Why are we focusing on gratitude? I believe everything is energy. In quantum physics, vibration means energy. All energy carries a vibration and a wavelength. When you place your attention on the wavelength of gratitude, that begins to be sent out into the Universe and will return to you in additional experiences that promote more gratitude.

Think of this process like a boomerang: you throw it into the Universe, and the Universe throws it right back. Instead of focusing on the wavelength you have been on for most of your life (not enough and pain), you are placing your awareness on gratitude.

As your past begins to peel away, you will become grateful for those experiences and able to understand the gifts in those situations. Your greater understanding will bring healing into all parts of you.

The pattern will begin to fade, because you are no longer trapped in the cycle of the pain. You can also ask yourself how this has served you, and then give thanks to that.

You may even realize that your body feels nothing—numb. Do not judge yourself. The awareness changes everything. Offer gratitude even when you think you feel or sense nothing.

This process of awareness is important for the liberation of stuck energy and as you move to the next two exercises.

The family issues have led to a misalignment of your Divine Mother/Father energy. These are directly tied into your connection with Creator, Universe, God, and Divine Intelligence.

Our Creator is One, embodying the feminine and masculine. Since you are created with this same energy, that means you embody both, too.

When you have imbalances, they will begin to show up over time in your physical body. In the next exercise, we begin to explore this more.

- **The Body**

This exercise will allow you to feel and see more clearly the imbalances in your physical body that are connected to your parental relationship

- Sit for a moment in silence while turning your attention to your physical body and notice how your body feels. (If you can sense pain, aches, dis-ease, discomfort, then move onto the next section. If not, skip down to the exercise that starts "no aches and pains.")
- Which side is the discomfort on? Does one side have more discomfort than the other side? Does this pain or ache associate with a memory or an experience?
- Are there any of the feelings/emotions stuck in your body? (Don't forget: you can refer back to the paragraph about the difference between emotions and feelings.) Where are the stuck feelings/emotions showing up in your body?
- Set the intention to liberate the energies stuck in your physical body.
- As you set the intention, if you feel an ache or discomfort, simply ask it to shift. You might want to talk to the ache and let it know how you feel and that

it is time to leave. Or just say to yourself, "I am ready for this to move out of my body now."

- The next step is to begin to move your body with a brisk walk, yoga, rebounder aka mini-trampoline, weight lifting, dancing to your favorite song, or any type of physical movement.
- During your movement, listen to what your body needs. Be sure to work both sides equally. (Working both sides of your body equally means you do exactly the same movement evenly on each side. Example: if you lift weights, make sure it is the same weight, reps, and sets for your right side and left side.)
- As you work both sides equally, state, "I liberate any and all energies that have been affecting my physical body. I Am in balance, both masculine and feminine now."

- **No Aches and Pains**

- Explore the right side of your body first by closing your eyes and bringing your awareness/attention to your foot. Notice any sensation as you bring your awareness to this part of your body. Do you get a color? Feeling? Thought? Word? Picture? Memory?
- Continue moving up your right side, exploring different body parts. Then repeat this on your left side.

- Did one side of your body provide you with more information than the other? If so, begin with this side of your body. If not, start with the left side of your body. Set the intention to liberate the energies that are stuck in your physical body.
- As you set the intention, if you can feel the ache, simply ask it to shift. You might want to talk to the ache and let it know how you feel and that it is time to leave. Or just say to yourself, "I am ready for this to move out of my body now."
- The next step is to begin to move your body with a brisk walk, yoga, rebounder aka mini-trampoline, weight lifting, or dance to your favorite song—any type of physical movement.
- During your movement, listen to what your body needs, and be sure to work both sides equally. As you work both sides equally, state, "I liberate any and all energies that have been affecting my physical body. I Am in balance, both masculine and feminine now."

- **Special note: If you have some distress connecting to your body**

If you are someone who feels disconnected from your body or in conflict with your body and this is causing fear or anxiety about conducting the body exercise, this tool supports creating a new relationship with your body.

- Begin by setting a timer for five minutes.
- Close your eyes while focusing on your breath as it comes in your body. Sense what breathing feels like to you as it goes in and out of your body.
- Then begin to move your body with a brisk walk, yoga, rebounder, weight lifting, dancing, or any type of physical movement.
- During your movement, listen to what your body needs, and be sure to work both sides equally. As you work both sides equally, state, "I liberate any and all energies that have been affecting my physical body. I Am in balance, both masculine and feminine now."

Some other signs that you are disconnected to your body:

- ✓ Overeating
- ✓ Undereating
- ✓ Mistreatment your body (mistreatment can be over-exercising and/or under-exercising, or having a strong dislike toward it.)

If you are experiencing fear to feel and be in your body, the key is to move from fear to a knowing that you are enough and are safe in your body. The human body is made up of energetic subatomic particles. What this means is, when you set your intention and move your body, things shift because energy follows intention.

My suggestion is to include these exercises in a regular practice. This will continue to release attachment to your experiences around your family of origin. Also, it helps if you welcome in feelings of neutrality and peace. Be patient with this process. Remember to offer your body gratitude.

A couple of metaphysical notes

All of the feelings/emotions that you have listed during these exercises are affecting your physical body. By completing these exercises, you are rewriting the pattern and its impact.

When you are in balance with your Divine Feminine, you are opening your receiving. This allows you to be more in the flow, to create and nurture with ease. The left side of your body represents the feminine.

When you are in balance with your Divine Masculine, this guides you to build structures that support you, to take action, and to provide for yourself and others. The right side of your body represents the masculine.

❖ The Spirit

This exercise will begin the deep, internal exploration and activation for change. It will allow you to connect with your own heart and begin to shift your energy from restricted, closed off, and unreceptive to deeply rooted into your Divine heart. When you are deeply connected to your heart, you are more open and ready to receive the support of your Soul.

- Sit in a comfortable position somewhere quiet.
- Take a deep breath, and feel the air as it comes into your body and exits.
- With each breath, your body begins to relax more and more.
- On your next breath, feel your heart expand in all directions: front, back, right, left, above, and below.
- Begin to notice a big mountain emerge within your heart center. This is the sacred mountain of your heart, which is solid and holds so much love.
- A beautiful vibrant color begins to emerge from the right side of this mountain. Feel it expand. Now, a beautiful vibrant color begins to emerge from the left side of this mountain. Feel it expand. Notice the colors begin to merge and move in harmony together.

- The colors begin to move down, connecting into the center of the Earth, while simultaneously moving up and connecting into the heart of Creator/God.
- Feel the Oneness from Creator/God merging with your colors and the sacred mountain of your heart.
- As this process is happening, all the disharmony within you that is connected with Divine Masculine and Feminine will begin to dissolve.
- Repeat to yourself: Creator activate balance to Oneness now.
- Sit in this stillness for as long as you feel you need.

Chapter 4

How is Not Enough Showing Up in Your Life?

YOU MIGHT BE AWARE of the not-enough pattern in your life, or it could be sneaky. We will explore more of what it looks and feels like and what makes this happen.

Let's dive in deeper to understand the depths of how not enough can affect every part of your life. What I have found is this can be very loud in one area of your life and very subtle in other areas.

For me, the loud area was my social life, as I was always trying to look perfect in my appearance to the point that it would take me hours to get ready to go out of my house. I was turning down opportunities to be social, because I felt like I did not have the right attire or enough time to pull my look together.

During this time, the subtlety was in my professional life. I was offered a position as head director of personal training at a gym. I did not step into that position, which I knew I would really excel at, because I did not feel I looked good enough for it. If I were to share this idea with anyone, that I didn't feel I looked good enough, they would have most likely disagreed, as my body was fit and strong. But *my image,* the one I felt I needed, in order to fit with that position, was having just ten-percent body fat and extremely defined muscles.

When you understand the subtleties, you can really begin to utilize your Divine power to make lasting changes.

As you begin to read the ways this can be expressed in the different areas of your life, my suggestion is to grab a notebook and write down what comes up for you. Write down things like feelings, thoughts, memories, and how your body feels while you read some of the following words.

Relationships and Not Enough

The not-enough impacts on relationships, how we present ourselves, how we react, and what we expect or don't.

In friendships, I would constantly compare myself to my friends. When I was younger, comparison was more about traits of the physical body. When I got older, even though my body comparisons were still there a bit, it took on a whole new level. Such as, "They have a better home... car... make more money... And their kids are scholars!"

There was a non-participation in my relationships, where I would stay quiet about voicing my opinion in certain situations. The one time I voiced my opinion about how I was being treated, I ended up losing my friend.

It still feels challenging to speak my truth and not care who agrees or disagrees. Bottom line: I would succumb to my friend's needs and wants just to keep a friend, even if it didn't feel right. I could never let them know my real thoughts and feelings.

In romance, recently I asked my husband of eleven years, "When I don't feel enough, what does this look like to you?"

He said, "You get guarded and defensive."

Until recently, I never understood what he meant. In the past, when he would bring this to my attention, I would feel deep anger and then tell him he did not know what he was talking about. I felt like every time I tried to express my deep feelings, the words were not heard, so I would get mad. This was the defensiveness he felt.

Every time he wanted to talk about something in our marriage that was not working, I would feel my body tighten up, as if I was getting my armor on and being guarded.

Now that I have moved into more of enoughness, I can see and understand what he means.

The thought process that created this defensive, guarded person was:

I would become guarded if, during a conversation with my husband, I felt like he wasn't listening to me and/or was telling me how I felt.

In the past, because I felt unworthy and to avoid conflict, I would become powerless in conversation. It was hard for me to engage in a conversation that might have conflict, because I felt like a loser most of the time anyway.

I pushed him away when I really wanted compassion and love. My unworthiness wouldn't allow me to receive what I wanted. During arguments, I wanted him to kiss me and tell me how beautiful I was, not talk through the conflict. I wanted to be shown love by his telling me how beautiful I was and physically showing me affection.

My internal dialogue was that I couldn't express myself because he would not hear me or be on my side.

One of the reasons I was so attracted to him was because he was a cheerleader for others. After we were married, my unworthiness and need for attention "told me" he was always helping others and never me. I couldn't put into words what I needed or even explain why I needed the things I did, like time to process.

My fear of being abandoned was always running, behind the scenes. I was just waiting for him to leave me, and I would often be mean and cruel to him to help the process along. This seems to have been a pattern in my life around love and friendships, that when I come to the realization I am ready to stand in my worthiness and be myself, they leave.

Where did all of this originate?

I believe this originated because, as a child, I witnessed my parents fighting most of the time.

In their new marriages, I witnessed my father being told by his partner how stupid he was after every statement he made, and my mother not speaking up for her own truth due to her depression—she would just shut down.

My father repeatedly asked me if I was telling the truth about being a survivor of rape and told me for many years I was making it up for attention.

My mother would not speak to me or even acknowledge me for weeks, and then, when I was a teenager, she berated me for my poor decisions.

All these feelings compounded during my first marriage, because my husband was a little hot-headed. When I spoke my feelings and shared my thoughts, I was shut down or he soothed me with gifts and treats.

A perfect illustration of this was when I got pregnant with my son. I was twenty-four years old and a starving actress living in New York City. When I told my son's father, who was my first husband, I was pregnant, he was so excited. He said, "Good. Now you can move back Upstate and live with me."

His excitement overshadowed all the thoughts I was trying to process and share, which included: How would I be a successful actress with a baby? Would my manager fire me? Would I be able to do both? Should I even have this child?

Not Enough and Its Many Faces

I want to provide you with examples of the many ways that not-enough shows up in our lives and our world.

Once again, I suggest you make little notations in the margin or in your journal about whatever resonates with you.

❖ In the Body

Your body is a highly evolved energetic vehicle that has been with you through every moment of your life. It holds memories and gives you subtle nudges when it needs something.

Think about it for a moment: if you had a traumatic physical fight with someone, your body carries the memory. Maybe it even gets flared up in those areas from time to time. For example, say you injured your right arm and the side of your face, and then you begin to suffer with psoriasis on that side of your body. You have an opportunity to pay attention to your body as it holds clues to your not feeling enough.

Janet had been married to John for over ten years. She had issues with her digestion and an intolerance to gluten and dairy. John came from an Italian family, so they ate pasta and cheese on a regular basis. They lived next door to John's family, and, being a family man, John and Janet ate with his family at least four nights a week.

This was very hard on Janet, because she wanted to show the family respect by eating what they prepared, but it had made her gain over thirty pounds. More importantly, it upset her stomach. When she brought up these concerns to her husband, he said he understood but did not make any changes.

Janet wanted to stay home more often and cook with her husband, because she was afraid of losing him. She didn't believe she deserved good health, so she didn't stand her ground.

Amy was on her second marriage of twelve years. In both of her marriages, her not-enoughness had impacted intimacy. She never felt like she was able to stand in her own power while being in a partnership.

Whenever disagreements occurred, she would feel tongue-tied and give up trying to express her deep feelings. The pool of not-enough just got deeper with each disagreement, and then it spilled over into the bedroom, as it was hard for her to be intimate with someone who she felt never allowed her the power of expression.

This directly impacted her vagina and it became red and itchy. When she went to doctors about this issue, they always told her she may have a bit of a yeast infection, but nothing showed up in the testing to explain her condition.

Karen was a stay-at-home mom with one child. Her partner was the primary provider financially. When they adopted their son, the plan of action Karen felt best was to keep up with the house work and have dinner ready for when her partner got home.

Every so often, when Karen came down with a virus or a cold, she just didn't have the energy to cook and clean-up. Even though her partner would have been fine with her taking some time to rest and recover, she never did. She did not feel enough for her own rest, recovery, and self-care.

❖ In the Financial Area

Everything around you has an energetic vibration, including your finances and money. Unfortunately, as young children, we can be taught that money is something we lack, and that belief generates fear of not enough. Your own relationship with money has family history and contains your family's beliefs and experiences. I have witnessed individuals who grow up with an over-abundance and yet still carry issues regarding their worth.

Some of the unsustainable beliefs associated with money are:

- ✓ money is evil
- ✓ money doesn't grow on trees
- ✓ the best things in life are free

When you place your enoughness outside of you and attach it to some item that responds to how you think and feel about it, you will always be chasing enough.

Phyllis was a brilliant researcher in the field of environmental studies. She was married once and never had any children. Her favorite pastime was to sit by the ocean and relax as the waves crashed against the shore.

Due to all the hours of research she put in at the lab for over twenty years, her body was tight, her joints were painful, and her balance was bad. This made it difficult for her to do many of the past things she loved, such as hiking.

Since she devoted so much time to work, she made an astronomical amount of money and never spent it. Despite knowing firsthand there were many companies and nonprofit organizations that could really benefit from donations, she never opened her wallet, due to her own feelings of not having enough. Deep inside, she had this fear of living long and running out of money. She did not feel like she ever had enough of it, yet if you spoke to her accountant or financial advisor, they would chuckle with disagreement.

Lisa worked for thirty years in a government job making good money yet not feeling fulfilled by her position. She was married to a man who took very good care of her financially and emotionally. They had two healthy boys who loved to buy things.

Lisa would go to the store every weekend and buy gifts for herself and the boys. She continued this pattern for many years, putting herself into debt and not sharing this debt with her husband. When her husband did find out about the outstanding debt from constant shopping, she was asked to stop. She agreed and did stop for a short time.

But Lisa's feelings of not enough did not allow her to stop for long. She once again started spending money and hid it from her husband. She continued this until her marriage was impacted. At that point, she had to take a good hard look at how money was filling her not-enough syndrome and affecting her life.

- **In the Spiritual Realm**

Many world religions contain rules and dogma that originally had a purpose. In some cases, the laws of that religion become more important than the purpose of spiritual connection. Often, individuals with "not enough" utilize any infraction or rule-breaking as a way to reinforce that they are not enough in the eyes of the Divine.

What they forget is God is an all-loving energy who resides inside everyone, and this God does not judge or criticize. Only humans do that. The placement of God/Creator outside of yourself exacerbates your not-enough syndrome.

Paula grew up with her grandparents, who were devout Catholics. She went to church every Wednesday, Saturday, and Sunday and attended an all-girls Catholic high school. Every night, when going to bed, Paula and her grandma would say their prayers out loud as they laid next to each other.

Paula felt her grandma was very faithful, and she truly believed her prayers were heard. All along, though, Paula used to quietly question why would God or any of the Angels listen to her? "They have so many more people out there in the world who are truly in need of help, more than little ole me." Paula's not-enough showed up by her praying for others and never herself.

❖ In the World

The evolution of humanity has utilized sex, color, and any difference in order to subdue others. For example, female energy has been looked upon as not-enough in society.

Women were not allowed to own property and were kept from positions of power and choice. Even in today's world, we often hear women are being paid less than others in the same position. Male energy of not enough can appear as men unable to communicate their feelings or being viewed as non-masculine, if they express their emotions freely. Men are often regarded as weak if they are vulnerable and show emotions. Men are left not knowing which way to turn and feeling inadequate, with no forum to express their feelings.

Marcie is eighty years young and has been retired from working as a medical assistant for over twenty years. From the stories she has shared with me, she was a spitfire during her career. Marcie spent over six years investing in her education and was a force to be dealt with at her job. During her career, she felt as if she had to work harder and smarter than the men of the company and noticed that promotions were handed out to men with less education and experience.

Her feelings of not-enough in the world resulted in Marcie's believing it wasn't "good enough" to be smart; you had to be beautiful, as well. During her twenties, a car accident resulted in scarring on the right side of her body. Her ankle was shattered during the accident, her thigh muscle was torn completely off, and her right shoulder cracked. She had surgery, and the only way they could repair her ankle was to fuse it into one position.

Marcie made the decision to have the doctors fuse her ankle in a position that would make wearing only high-heeled shoes possible. Her thigh had a plate placed in it, which left a large lump that would show if she wore a skirt above the knee. She was fine with the fusion of her ankle, as she thought women should always wear high-heeled dress shoes. But she refused to wear certain clothes because she was embarrassed by the plate in her thigh, as it no longer looked like the images in magazines.

When I asked her about letting society's views go and dropping her guard, in order to do what she felt comfortable with, she looked down at the ground, gave me a little giggle, and said, "I am too old for change now."

- **With food**

Hippocrates said, "Let food be thy medicine and medicine be thy food." Unfortunately, individuals in not-enough are using food to self-medicate their pain and as a way to feel in control.

The self-medicators for pain will overeat food that is not life-giving when they are stressed, sad, lonely, or just feeling the everyday not-enoughs. The controllers will use food by withholding intake.

My Affair with Food

During my formative years, when I was feeling "fat," I would starve myself. This feeling of fatness was usually triggered when I had conflicts or disagreements in my life. At that time, I didn't have the skills to discover or make the connection between my feelings and my food deprivation. I was literally trying to starve my feelings away.

One episode of starvation came after a night out with my best friend and a group of boys. On the ride home from a movie, I closed my eyes for a minute, and my best friend obviously thought I was asleep, because she began talking about me. This really close friend of mine told these guys I was a tease, not funny, and overall not good enough. I starved myself all day until I couldn't take it anymore, and then I binge ate.

The result of binge eating put my body into another kind of distress, and the entire experience proved to me, in my mind, that I wasn't good enough. Now, years later, I understand that my girlfriend also felt not enough, and this was her way of expressing it.

Becky had chores growing up, like most kids. The one chore she loathed was dishes, because she had to do them every day. Her siblings were not required to do chores, so there seemed to be a never-ending stack of dishes for Becky.

When Becky went to college, she noticed she gained more than the Freshman 15 and began to pay more attention to what she was putting into her mouth and why.

She realized that every time she had to do the dishes, she went to the cabinet and snapped off a piece of dark chocolate. She noticed that the chocolate was a response to her feeling alone and not-enough while doing dishes as a child.

Rika was a single mom of two young girls. She did not get much down time, due to work and parenting. Once a month, her mom would watch the girls while she went out for a few hours.

Rika was shy and had a small circle of friends, so her go-to companion on her nights out was her cousin. They usually would grab a bite to eat and either walk around the mall or see a movie. Her cousin was a Negative Nellie, always complaining about how hard life was for her. Even though Rika loved her cousin, she found her to be toxic, and every time she got home, she would binge eat on anything she could find.

Everything her cousin said stirred up all her fears and feelings of potential failure, so overeating provided her momentary joy and solved the problem for a short period of time.

- **With Exercise**

Intense exercise is another way to control how you are feeling around not-enough.

Throughout my youth, I would try to exercise my feelings out of me. If I had an argument with a boyfriend, I would run hard and fast until my legs collapsed. I had no process to digest the intense feelings within me, so I would divert my attention by torturing my body.

Also, the over-exercise provided me with a vision on how to solve my not-enough. If my body was amazing and picture-perfect, all the boys would want me. I was creating a no-win situation in my life: I felt horrible if I didn't exercise and also if I did.

❖ At Work

For those of us who feel not enough, you might be utilizing parts of your life to prove you are enough. Work and career are an excellent playing field for this. They can highlight the perfect storm of not-enough factors: money, success, and status. Just like money, work, too, has a lot of belief paradigms around it.

Lizzie was a CEO at a financial firm. She started working around age eleven and never stopped. Most of her friends and coworkers commended her on her work ethic, no matter what job or position she held. She told me she always put extra time into projects and always went the extra mile.

No matter how many accolades she received from her boss, Lizzie always felt that she could have done better. She admitted how she never felt satisfied with her performance and projects.

As we worked together, I started her on the *Eating to Enough* meal guide, and, as she followed the simple plan, her clarity grew around not-enough and work. She realized she never felt enough in the workplace because she was indirectly looking to feel enough in her father's eyes. Her father was a savvy, successful business man for the majority of his life. Lizzie was just as talented as her father and was still waiting for the approval of her father to truly accept that.

There is a drive in you to go all out and shine in the workplace that, over time, leads to exhaustion and burnout. If you continue to ignore this, eventually your body batteries run low and adrenal fatigue begins, as happened to Lizzie. This may also lead to tight muscles and/or chronic muscle spasms.

Metaphysically, your muscles hold the structure of your life together. If you are giving 120% to your career, which directly affects all the other areas of your life, and you are not allowing for flexibility, your muscles will begin to talk to you. Adrenal fatigue is a signal that you are pushing your life force in only one direction harder and harder, when what your body really needs, is balance in work, rest, and play.

In the Spotlight and Not Enough

There is a calling to be in the spotlight, but for those who believe that fame, fortune, and status will solve the not enough syndrome, it won't. If you are trying to fill a hole, being in the spotlight can only exacerbate what you are already feeling within. You will always have people who disagree with your views, or who pick apart your lifestyle and your physical appearance.

After I graduated performing arts college, I lived in Manhattan so I could go on auditions. I was looking to get picked for the next big part. I had this feeling, if I could "make it there," I would feel whole and complete.

One day, I landed an audition for a national hair commercial. I was so excited! This could be my big break. I knew my hair was beautiful, because several times a day people complimented its thickness, curls, and length.

The day of the audition, I took extra care picking out my wardrobe, including a bright-blue shirt that matched the color of my eyes. I walked into a room filled with girls who looked very similar to me. An uncomfortable stillness loomed while we all waited to see who was the chosen one. During my audition, after I read my part, one of the "judges" stared at me a said, "Well, honey, you are no Ford model."

All of my not-enoughness came rushing to the top. I didn't have the internal defenses to stare him down. I was crushed. I said to him, "I know I am not a Ford model." Then I stood there, my head dropped in embarrassment, feeling like I wanted to crawl up in a hole and hide away forever. Every single part of me in that moment felt not enough. Not enough to ever have a big role.

This man had called out my innermost demons. He reflected to me exactly what I felt inside. I realized I could no longer even fake it, as my not-enough was felt by others, and in order for me to step into the spotlight, I had to do some inner work.

With God/Creator and Not Enough

When a baby is born, it does not know how to compare itself to another baby. Actually, just thinking of one baby comparing itself to another sounds a bit silly, yet, as adults, we do it all of the time.

In today's society, with our social media craze, everyone is sharing only the highlights of their life, which makes them look so blessed. This creates more comparison, competition, and envy. It's creating a falsified mirror of lack, and many people are looking into it all the time.

When you focus continuously on your shortcomings, you will keep fracturing the organic connection you have with yourself. Over time, you will distance yourself from where you came from, separating yourself from God/Creator, because you feel like you are nothing and God is everything. You began in this world as a baby, just like the rest of us, which makes you pure love, God.

Danica was in a session with me when we were talking about how she wanted her body to release thirty pounds. I asked her to get curious with me, as curiosity is the cure for judgment. I began by asking her questions such as, "What do you really want? What would losing pounds do for you? Who would you become, if you were thirty pounds lighter?"

Then, all of a sudden, it was as if we broke a seal. She began to say, "I don't deserve to release thirty pounds... I don't deserve anything."

I said, "Of course you do, because you are a part of the Divine/God."

She said, "I don't believe that. I am not deserving to be a part of God."

It didn't surprise me that she couldn't transform her body, because she was trying to do all the work by herself and forgot that, with Divinity, everything is possible. Up until that point, she did not even realize she was not connected to God.

Today, she not only prays for herself but for others as well.

Why does this happen?

It could come from a narcissistic parent who didn't show love in the ways you needed. They only give you praise when you are doing things that interest them. Having a parent who does not allow you to have a different opinion or a voice of your own will shut you down; they will tell you you don't know anything. If you don't feel like you are worth much and you are told your voice is useless by your parent, who else will disagree? After all, parents are supposed to be our first line of love in this world, our comfort, and safety.

They may even have compared you to other children, pointing out your flaws and wishing you could be different, instead of looking at your strengths and keeping the focus there for you to thrive.

Maybe your parent had their own childhood traumas that were never dealt with, so they were left feeling emotionally distant and unattached.

Here is a big one: maybe your parent did not feel good enough, and so *you* began to model that behavior, because they were your role model. Or maybe your parent was an overachiever, and you just could not walk in the same big shoes.

It could come from having a sibling who put you down and beat you up. Or even an experience with a best friend who stabbed you in the back. You could have experienced a personal trauma of sexual abuse.

We could take this to a whole other level and say it may even come in from a past life, as your soul lives out unresolved karma. It even could be in your zodiac chart. Sometimes, mine sure does feel like that.

We can say this comes from outside sources and blame them all day, but that will never get you resolution. I decided a long time ago, if I kept blaming my parents and my traumas for my never feeling good enough, I would stay paralyzed in the past and never be able to move forward in my life.

My mom struggled with depression and my dad had his own self-worth issues, but at the end of the day, after I took time to work through the mental and emotional baggage I held against them, I realized they did the best they could in that time of their lives. It is not up to me to fix them. It is up to me to find my inner Light and work with that daily to put myself in a place of expansion.

Why Is This Happening for You?

You have now read some scenarios and how not-enough expresses in other's lives. Below is a list of questions you might consider to further determine how "not enough" is manifesting in your life.

Questions:

- ✓ Am I self-medicating with food?
- ✓ Am I giving too little or too much in my friendships?
- ✓ Do I believe my partner will leave me one day?

- ✓ Do I believe I am attractive enough to date and marry?
- ✓ Do I deserve the body I desire?
- ✓ Why am I silent during disagreements?
- ✓ Am I starving my body to change?
- ✓ Why would God love me?
- ✓ Why would God help me?
- ✓ Do I feel God resides within me?
- ✓ Do I feel like I have to prove myself in the workplace?
- ✓ Do I always have to outsmart and one-up others?
- ✓ Is my debt a direct link to my not enoughness?
- ✓ Are my thoughts overpowering my life decisions?
- ✓ Am I creating distractions instead of actively taking action toward my big dreams?
- ✓ Do I have work-life perfectionism?
- ✓ Am I not good enough if I can't give 120%?
- ✓ When I do give 120%, do I feel it could be better?
- ✓ Am I overdriven in the workplace and do I feel burned out and exhausted, yet I keep pushing myself?

A Couple of Last Thoughts about Sneaky Ways of Not Enough

On your way home from work, you stop at the grocery store to pick up dinner. You end up buying food you don't need, such as Twinkies and caramel-covered popcorn, because you had a challenging day.

You make a nice dinner for your partner, and they don't appreciate your hard work as they sit there complaining about their friends. Not once do they stop and say thank you. You binge eat on the chocolate dessert you baked.

You go shopping for clothes and spend over your limit, putting yourself into credit card debt, because you are going on a date.

Your kids and husband are out of town for the weekend. You put on a movie while eating your dinner. You realize halfway through the movie that you ate the entire pizza and want something else now.

You have a closet full of clothes that are oversized.

You love making new friends. Actually, you have a large collection of them but don't really know them well.

Your find yourself sharing other people's quotes on social media instead of sharing your own thoughts and feelings.

You are concerned if you upset someone when driving. You make a right turn and realize it was not correct, but you feel terrible having to slow down and affect the traffic behind you in order to get yourself turned around. You end up driving out of your way to turn around, just so you don't upset other drivers.

You internally judge someone upon meeting them for the first time.

You immediately compliment someone back when they give you a compliment first.

You react instead of responding to someone in connecting with them and the story they share with you.

Chapter 5

Transformation

TRANSFORMATION IS A process that we are all undergoing, whether we are aware of it or not. From the moment we were conceived, we have been in a transformation process. Our cells create a very intricate body that undergoes a change every seven to ten years. Our skin cells change every two to three weeks, and the ones in our gut every five days. It truly is innate for us to move through transformation.

In Richard Rudd's book, *The Gene Keys,* he writes about transformation being a three-part process: survival, service, surrender. When in the survival phase, you are operating on a level based mostly in fear. In the service phase, you have moved past survival fear enough to bring your gifts to serve humanity. The surrender phase is giving up all identities that don't serve you and becoming a full manifestation of your Divinity.

Transforming from not enough to enough can and does happen. At times, it will feel like you are not getting anywhere, because transformation does not happen overnight. It is a slow and steady process you are forever mastering. You begin in a place of just coping with life, knowing you have challenges from past experiences that you allow to define you. You transform into a place of understanding; the challenges have an impact on your decisions, but you begin to make new choices consciously for change.

Each choice begins a new story and creates new feelings of excitement in your life. Finally, you will feel confident in your decisions and your life, because you have let go of the limitations you placed on yourself and you are now co-creating with the Divine. It feels as if all the chains you were once in have broken off, and you are set free to create, dance, sing, play, and explore life and all of its opportunities.

Recently, I went to a weekend business seminar, where I was one of twenty women. The biggest take-away for me was not business information but a deep knowledge of how much I have transformed.

I made a choice to take myself out of my comfort zone by not asking any of my friends or colleagues to join me. Another way I challenged myself was the event was two hours away and I drove myself.

When I walked into this place, I felt as though I could conquer the world! In the past, I would have pulled my energy in and gotten very quiet. I would have contemplated to blend in and hide, because my thoughts of not-enough would have been telling me everyone there was more successful than I.

But, this time, I felt I deserved to be there just as much as the next woman. As the seminar progressed, I had insight into questions that other women asked, and I raised my hand and gave my opinion. For the first time in my life, it really did not matter to me if anyone agreed or not. It just felt amazing to speak what was right and true to me.

At the end of the day, we were asked to do an exercise that was all about being seen and being vulnerable. You have to look into someone's eyes and say nothing for at least a minute. Not only did I have to do this once, but they had us paired up with at least ten women. Though that exercise was not my favorite, I felt so solid in doing it. At the end of this, a woman came up to me and said, "You have done massive amounts of inner work. You are ready to take your business to the next level."

This was the first time in my life I have been in a room full of women who were also business entrepreneurs and felt so strong, alive, and confident in myself. This doesn't mean my transformation is over, as I do believe it is a lifelong process.

But it was freaking awesome to see and feel how much I have shifted. I truly believe you can do the same—it just takes practice and patience with yourself each day.

So, how do you begin your practice of transformation? In this chapter, I will provide you different exercises for the mind, body, and spirit.

The plan is made simple for you. I have broken it down week by week. I suggest, as you practice, you journal daily about your experiences, your thoughts, and your feelings.

At the end of ninety days, go over your journal and write yourself a letter to see how far you come. (You can check out the easy blueprint of the process at the end of this book.)

After your ninety days, you can continue the practice, or you can use the exercises of maintenance when you experience a not-enough situation.

90 Days to Enough Plan Basics

❖ Mindset and Enough

Think of a plastic water bottle. If the plastic water bottle sits in a car on a hot sunny day, you can feel the plastic as soft, and, with a gentle squeeze, it becomes pliable. Science confirms that your brain is very similar to this water bottle, as it has the same plasticity. It is called neural plasticity, which is the ability of the brain to change throughout a person's lifetime.

Every day, experiences shape and mold your brain. This is powerful news, because it is scientific proof that we can change habits, behaviors, and patterns that do not serve our growth and evolution.

According to Michael Merzenich, in the book, *The Brain that Changes Itself*, "practicing ... a new habit under the right conditions, can change hundreds of millions and possibly billions of the connections between the nerve cells in our neural pathways."

Research has shown that when you focus on experiences, practices, and situations that make you happy, a specific part of your brain is stimulated. As this stimulation keeps happening, your brain gets stronger on feeling happy, and it begins to solidify new pathways. Every thought you think and every feeling that comes with that thought begins to create a pathway.

That means, by now, by feeling not-enough, you have a pathway of not-enough wired in your brain, and it is time to change it. This is a process that takes a bit of time, because you have to first create a new pathway and then you must continue to stimulate that pathway for it to strengthen. If you do this consistently, however, what eventually happens is that old pathways begin to fade and no longer fire.

In 1949, Donald Hebb, a Canadian psychologist who was influential in the area of neuropsychology, discovered that "neurons that fire together wire together."

How do you create new pathways? I will share with you the top exercises that have worked for me and my clients. All of them come down to a 3-step formula, which is:

1) Forming
2) Strengthening
3) Solidifying

1. Forming

In order to begin to form a new pathway, it is vital that you have awareness. For thirty-five years of my life, I had a touch of awareness, I knew I was stuck in a pattern of sabotage, yet I had no idea I could stop the mind from going down the same pathway.

That is until one sunny summer day, when it all clicked. I was driving, and it was eighty degrees outside. My windows were down, and I was on a beautiful country road filled with many gorgeous flowers. I came to the end of the road and realized I did not remember half my ride. What was I thinking? Where was my mind?

I made a deal with myself: for the next two weeks, I was going to be in the present moment. During those two weeks, every few minutes, I would stop myself and notice where my thoughts were and what my mind was doing. After a few days, I started to set my alarm on my phone to go off every fifteen minutes, so I could stop and access my thoughts.

This very exercise was how I began to realize I was playing stories and scenarios in my head of the many ways I was not enough. It was abuse. I was fermenting in my past. I would notice I was thinking of my past and certain situations when I felt not enough. I noticed I would play a scenario about an argument with my husband over and over, not feeling enough. Every thought was full of "could haves" and "should haves."

Once I started this awareness of pausing in any given moment to take note of where my mind was, life began to transform. I had the power to change my mind in every moment.

This is how I developed the *Resetting Your Mind* exercise, and why I use it to begin the journey to enoughness.

2. Strengthening

To create a new pathway of enoughness in your mind, you must strengthen that route with perseverance and persistence.

It is important to understand why you want your thoughts to shift. This will allow you to continue to focus and keep you on the path.

In the first few years of my second marriage, we had many bumps in the road. We were both struggling to provide for the household and, with a new baby, my not enough was louder than ever. The extra weight and being sleep-deprived also contributed to my not-enough syndrome, along with our living in a small apartment (with a family of four) and not a house.

I often felt alone. The dialogue with my husband went from pre-married deep conversations about our feelings to who would buy the toilet paper and diapers.

I yearned for that connection again with my husband. A marriage that was open with communication and mutually supportive was what I wanted back very deeply. My marriage was my deeper "why." Why I wanted to strengthen the new connections in my brain and knowing this made me persevere to make a change. The questions below helped me get to my big why. When it is rooted in your heart, you will persist until transformation happens in the brain.

3. Solidifying

Have you taken the same route to work daily? After a while, you go into autopilot on your route—like a zombie, zoned out, or talking on the phone, just going through the motions. Then, one day, there is a detour, and you are forced to change the route. Now you have to pay full attention. This new route creates an awareness in you, and you become more alert driving to work than you have been in a while.

This is what happens when you struggle with not enough. You are on autopilot. Once you become fully aware (formation) and understand your big why (strengthening), now you can take an action step to retrain the brain on its new route. Your brain wants to work efficiently, so the most used pathway (the one with the least resistance) is what your brain will use.

In order to solidify the new behavior, you have to work your brain daily. It takes twenty-one to twenty-eight days to form a new habit. Some researchers even say it takes sixty-six days to really lock in new brain pathways. As Buddha taught, "What you think you become." This is very true about your enoughness. *Think enough, become enough.*

One of the best ways to solidify new pathways is with meditation. This practice takes your brain out of stress and survival mode and puts it into rest and rejuvenation mode. Researchers from Yale and Harvard have discovered that meditation alters the structure and function of the brain.

I started meditating when I was seventeen years old, when I began to study metaphysics. I remember the first time I sat down to meditate on my own. I lit candles, burned incense, and put on some sort of slow instrumental music, then I tried to sit in that weird pretzel position. First, my legs went numb and my back was screaming. I did not last more than five minutes. My mind was running like crazy, thinking about what I had to do. If I had to give you a description of what it was like in my head, I would say the closest thing to describing my first meditation was a bad hard-rock concert, where the music is too loud, the speakers thumping, and the band is screaming lyrics. I could not find any kind of peace.

I found the secret is to keep doing it. It is called a practice for a reason. It takes a lot of practice to find your quiet. You are not doing anything wrong when you begin and your mind is on the hamster wheel. Don't give up. Try it for three minutes a day and then increase to five minutes. Keep adding time as you feel ready. It helps a lot when you can focus on your breathing and a mantra. I have provided a mantra for you to follow in meditation below, in the instructions for Month Three.

- **Food Focus Support**

To become clearer in your mind, we are going to use the support of food. The reason it is best to avoid the items below is because they are known to create inflammation in the body. If your body is inflamed, it is working overtime and is not in its natural resting state, which makes it challenging to get full rejuvenation. These items also create brain fog. Once you get them out of your system, your brain becomes clearer and you have an opportunity to see the deeper truths in yourself and in your life.

Foods that are overly processed can also create feelings of separation. The degree of separation between the growth of the food and when it hits your table is vast, and your intuitive nature will feel that, whether you are conscious of it or not.

It is best to avoid any processed foods (foods that are in a box, frozen, or have more than five ingredients).

It is also best to avoid any processed sugars, which are any and all sweeteners except raw honey or pure maple syrup.

The most important thing to focus on during this flush is eating whole foods. For example, the ingredients in a potato or a strawberry is one: potato and strawberry! There are many great recipes on the Internet that are easy and only use a few ingredients.

The intention is to flush out the toxins in our body so we can fully embrace forgiveness.

Increasing your water intake to half your body weight in ounces would be very helpful, too, as this will also flush out toxins even more rapidly. For example, if you currently weigh

120 pounds, then drinking sixty ounces of fresh, plain water daily is your goal. Tea, seltzer, or anything else except water does not count.

❖ Body Movement Support

Get that heart pumping. When we conduct cardio, your heart works harder, pumping blood through your system quicker. The heart expands and the blood moves the toxins through your system. Sweating will also help release the toxins through your skin.

It is recommended, in order to achieve a solid increase in your heart rate, to conduct a thirty to forty-minute cardio session.

Depending on your stamina, you can begin with walking, if you are not already exercising on a daily basis. If you already participate in a regular exercise program, then challenge yourself by jogging or walking up a hill. Your goal is to increase your heart rate. The way to gauge this is to feel challenged and slightly breathless, yet you are still able to talk normally.

Chapter 6

90 Days to Enoughness Plan

EACH OF THE 90 days, you want to:

- See if that day or week has any special instructions and conduct those exercises
- Select a movement exercise each day (this is in addition to cardio)
- Utilize the *Food to Enough* food selection section each day

Week One

- **Day 1**

- **Special Instructions: Resetting Your Mind**

Set an alarm to go off every fifteen minutes. When the alarm goes off, immediately stop what you are doing and notice what your mind was focusing on. If it is focused on what you have done wrong, that you are not good enough, then take your focus to a time in your life when you felt good.

Forgiveness Flush

In continuing to heal from the trauma of sexual abuse, I would attend a therapy session or church or read a passage where the message was I "needed" to forgive. This word haunted me for many years. I would become agitated, thinking about forgiveness: how do I forgive someone who did something so bad?

I began to say to myself, well, I can forgive, but I certainly cannot forget. For a while, this put a Band-Aid over the wound, yet I still felt like I did not understand or was even close to forgiving.

Forgiveness is a process and a practice that takes time to really soak into your heart and mind. When you are in the consciousness of forgiveness and the situation is no longer emotionally charged, then you can make decisions based on the consciousness of neutrality. Then you can consciously choose to have your words and actions anchored in peace.

Day 1—Forgiving others

- **Timeline Review**

Set aside fifteen to twenty minutes with a journal, and go back in time as far back as your mind can take you. Begin by writing down who you feel you need to forgive. People who may have said things to hurt you. People who may have made choices to hurt you physically. People who hurt others you cared for.

Continue the writing and reflecting process until you feel there is no more at this moment to discover. You are complete once you get to the current age you are now.

After your list is complete, begin your cardio. Before beginning cardio, say this: "I allow my body to liberate what it has stored from the memories of all the people I feel I would like to forgive."

At bedtime, close your eyes, and ask for the golden light of purity and peace to saturate you while you sleep.

- **Day 2**

➢ **Special Instructions: Forgiving yourself**

Timeline Review

Set aside fifteen to twenty minutes with a journal and go back in time as far back as your mind can take you. Begin by writing down what makes you feel as though you need forgiveness. Times when you may have said things hurtful things to others. Situations you may have made choices to hurt others physically.

Continue the writing and reflecting process until you feel there is no more at this moment to discover. You are complete once you get to the current age you are now.

After your list is complete, begin your cardio. Before beginning cardio, say this: "I allow my body to liberate what it has stored from the moments I have hurt myself or anyone else."

At bedtime, close your eyes, and ask for the golden light of purity and peace to saturate you while you sleep.

- **Day 3: Resetting Your Mind**

➢ **Special Instructions: Forgiving God/Creator/Universe**

Timeline Review

Set aside fifteen to twenty minutes with a journal, and go back in time as far back as your mind can take you. Write down the things for which you feel you need to forgive God. Continue the writing and reflecting process until you feel there is no more at this moment to discover. You are complete once you get to the current age you are now.

After your list is complete, begin your cardio. Before beginning cardio, say this: "I allow my body to liberate what it has stored from the moments I created and chose separation from God/Creator."

At bedtime, close your eyes, and ask for the golden light of purity and peace to saturate you while you sleep.

###

By the fourth day, you should be feeling complete with this process and a lot lighter physically, mentally, emotionally. Some people have even lost a few pounds doing this. If you feel you need to repeat the process, you can begin the exercise starting over from day one. Each time you do this, you are able to go deeper. Remember: transformation is like an onion that has many layers to peel away.

This incorporates the body, mind, and spirit. Along with the daily exercise, it is also suggested that you support your body with food and movement.

- **Days 4, 5, 6, 7 and the rest of the month: Resetting Your Mind**
- **Special Instructions**

Keep practicing the Resetting Your Mind exercise, along with the other parts of the program.

Month 2

- **Special Instructions**

Today, you will move from Resetting Your Mind to the Strengthening exercise.

- **Strengthening**

Let's understand the deeper meaning, so you can help your mind strengthen.

Grab a pen and paper, and take a few minutes to answer the questions below. My suggestion is to begin with the one area of your life where your not-enough syndrome is the loudest or most predominant.

1. What do I want or what would I like?

Example: I would like a stronger connection with my husband, a better relationship. A relationship where I feel enough.

2. What will having that do for me?

Example: It will bring an overall sense of peace and make me feel secure in being myself. It will allow me to travel in business more without feeling neglectful. It will put my mind at peace that he will not stray and cheat.

3. How will I know when I have it? (Be very specific here. What will you see, hear, and feel?)

Example: I will see us having more meaningful conversations, where we are deeply connecting with our words. I am able to express myself fully without holding back my feelings due to fear. I hear us laughing more. I feel joy in my heart, and we are intimate more often.

4. When, where, and with whom do I want it?

Example: I want it with my husband, and I want it to begin tonight when he gets home from work.

5. How will having this outcome affect other people? (Another way to ask this for yourself is what is the consequence to you and all the people in your life?)

Example: It will bring joy to me and help my husband feel more connected, which will bring down his daily irritation. It will also have an effect on our children, as they will witness better communication, which will set them up for success in the future with relationships.

6. What (if anything) might you have to let go of that you value, if you were to follow through?

Example: The old hurts from past relationships. My pride and walls that guard my heart. Staying safe in my non-communicating comfort zone. Even some of my alone time at night, when I usually read and relax.

7. What might open up for you, if you make a change?

Other relationships changing and getting stronger, plus healthy boundaries for me so I feel more energized daily versus depletion.

- **Month 3**

➢ **Special Instructions**

As you are approaching your last month, you are moving into solidifying your new brain pathways.

Solidifying

Actions daily and meditation will help...

There are two actions I took to create new pathways. One was with meditation, and the other was literally making different choices daily that took me a bit out of my comfort zone. This one I called breaking the glass ceiling.

The Breaking Glass Ceiling Plan.

I suggest you start meditating for three minutes a day and then increase to five minutes. Keep adding time as you feel ready. It helps a lot when you can focus on your breathing and a mantra. I have provided a mantra for you to follow in meditation below, in the instructions for month three.

➢ Your mantra while you sit in meditation is I AM ENOUGH.

➢ Breath in and say to yourself, I am enough.

➢ Breath out and say to yourself, I am enough

➢ Set your timer for three minutes and go.

If you are an avid meditator, you can follow this:

- Start in a seated position with your feet placed on the floor. Close your eyes, and bring awareness to your breath. Begin to breathe in, and say to yourself, "I am enough." As you breathe out, you say to yourself, "I am enough."
- Bring your awareness to the top of your head, the crown chakra, as you breathe in. Feel your breath going straight into this chakra as you say, "I am enough." You feel this chakra opening, and it is now gently spiraling in a clockwise direction.
- Bring your awareness in between your eyebrows, the third eye chakra, as you breathe in. Feel your breath going straight into this chakra as you say, "I am enough." You feel this chakra opening, and it is now gently spiraling in a clockwise direction.
- Bring your awareness to your neck/throat area, the throat chakra, as you breathe in. Feel your breath going straight into this chakra as you say, "I am enough." You feel this chakra opening, and it is now gently spiraling in a clockwise direction.
- Bring your awareness to your chest area, the heart chakra, as you breathe in. Feel your breath going straight into this chakra as you say, "I am enough." You feel this chakra opening, and it is now gently spiraling in a clockwise direction.

- Bring your awareness to your solar plexus, the solar plexus chakra, as you breathe in. Feel your breath going straight into this chakra as you say, "I am enough." You feel this chakra opening, and it is now gently spiraling in a clockwise direction.
- Bring your awareness to your belly below your naval, the sacral chakra, as you breathe in. Feel your breath going straight into this chakra as you say, "I am enough." You feel this chakra opening, and it is now gently spiraling in a clockwise direction.
- Bring your awareness to the base of your spine, the root chakra, as you breathe in. Feel your breath going straight into this chakra as you say, "I am enough." You feel this chakra opening, and it is now gently spiraling in a clockwise direction.
- As all of your chakras are now in harmony with your "I am enough," begin to imagine a platform. There are three steps leading to the top of this platform. As you take the first step of I, second step of Am, and third step Enough, you are now standing on your platform of enoughness.

  Notice what color it is. Maybe it is more than one color. Allow these colors to soak into all parts of you.
- Now, bring remembrance of your Divine nature, which is more than enough. Stay here as long as you feel you

need. When complete, begin to feel this platform absorb into all areas of your body.

- Bring your awareness back to the room you are in. Feeling your feet on the ground, begin to move your body around, bringing yourself back to being very grounded and present in the moment now.

- **Movement to Enough**

In quantum physics, everything is energy. This includes the physical vessel you call your body. The body is made up of nine systems:

1. Circulatory
2. Endocrine
3. Respiratory
4. Reproductive
5. Digestive
6. Muscular
7. Nervous
8. Urinary
9. Skeletal

When you break these systems down, they are made up of organs and tissues. The organs and tissues are made up of cells. The cells are made up of molecules, and the molecules are made up of atoms. Atoms are made up of subatomic particles, which are energy.

This brings me to what Einstein said: "Energy cannot be created or destroyed, it can only be changed from one form to another." Keeping in mind Einstein's statement, that would mean the particles that make up your body can be affected by the energy of not-enough, and you can transform this by rearranging those particles.

Every part of your body has a spiritual meaning behind it. I have selected the main body parts that connect to your not-enough, so you can begin to shift this with intention and movement. These are easy moves that can be done almost anywhere.

✶ Jumping Jack Squat Combo: Ignite Enough

When you do not feel enough, you have a tendency to guard your heart and collapse your energy, because you feel small. Increasing your heart rate with movement will open your heart center and allow your energy to expand, so you can feel more in your power. Incorporating the legs allows you to ground in this feeling of expansion and worthiness. Your legs represent moving your enoughness forward and having balance in all areas of your life while doing it.

The Exercise:

- Start by standing with your feet together and your arms by your sides.

- Simultaneously jump both feet apart and bring both arms out to the sides, reaching your hands up to the sky. Jump back to starting position.
- Repeat 10 times
- (If you need to modify, jump only right leg and arm out and in then the left side. Continue alternating, until you completed 10 jacks on each side.)
- Without a rest, go straight into the next part of the exercise: the squats
- Stand up tall with your head facing forward and with your shoulders relaxed and down. Have your feet shoulder-width apart. Move your body down, as if you are sitting in a chair.
- Stand back up to start position
- Repeat 10 times.
- (If you need to modify this, you can use a chair, standing and sitting on and off the chair.)
- Start again with the jumping jack part of the exercise
- Repeat both parts 3 times

- **Push-Up One Arm Chest Tap: Embrace Enough**

This exercise not only strengthens the chest and arms, but it brings balance to both masculine and feminine energies. It specifically targets the chest muscles, which support your ability to feel safe in love. The breast area represents nurturing, as this is how babies are meant to be fed and nourished. The arms are about embracing life at its fullest. When you feel enough, you open your arms wide to receive, because you feel deserving of it.

- ➢ Start on a mat in push-up position on the floor, with your hands slightly wider than your shoulders
- ➢ Curl your toes under, so you come up on the balls of your feet and your whole body lifts off the floor.
- ➢ Bend your elbows as you lower your torso toward the floor then straighten the elbows back to your beginning position.
- ➢ Once you are back to your start position, take your right hand and tap the left side of your chest. Place your right hand back on the floor. Now, the left hand touches the right chest and goes back to the floor.
- ➢ Repeat, starting from the pushup position, 10 times.
- ➢ (If you need to modify this, place your knees on the floor while doing your pushup. The closer your knees are to your chest, the easier it will be. The farther away they are from your chest, the harder it will be. If you can't get on the floor, you can do this with your hands on a wall.)

- ✶ **Plank: Align Enough**

This exercise strengthens the very deep core muscles near your spine.

Your abdominal area is the core of your inner knowing and creativity. It's where you get the signal of your gut responses. If this is clogged up with not-enough, you are in denial of your truth—that you are whole and beautiful. Doing this exercise will strengthen your truth, inner knowing, and creativity. Since these core muscles connect to your spine, this will also allow you to stay in the alignment of enough.

- Place your hands on the ground directly underneath your shoulders.
- Bend at the elbow so you come down onto your forearms, creating a 90-degree angle in the elbow area.
- Tuck your toes under, and lift your body off the ground, so the only areas touching the ground are your forearms and your toes.
- Your body should be in a tabletop position as you hold this for 30 seconds.
- Repeat two more times.
- (If you need to modify this, you can bring your knees to the ground and hold. Or you can use the back of a chair, by placing your hands on the chair and walking your feet out behind you a bit until your body is at an angle. Hold this for 30 seconds)
- As this gets easier to hold, you can begin to increase the time you hold.

✶ Seated Twist: Express Enough

This exercise brings strength and flexibility to your mid-section.

Your mid-section, which is located in your abdominal area, stores many of your vital organs. All of your organs connect with different emotions: the liver is connected with anger, the kidneys with shame. This part of your body is how you deal with and process your emotions. Do you suppress or express? Many emotions can couple with not-enough, such as shame, blame, guilt, and fear.

When you don't feel enough, you either suppress your emotions or you express them by reacting instead of responding. Moving this area of your body will allow you to express by responding.

- Start seated on the floor with your knees bent, your feet on the ground, and your heels about twelve inches from your glutes.
- Lean back slightly until you feel your belly engage, keeping your back straight.
- Place your arms straight out in front of you, with your hands on top of each other.
- Your hands should be level with the bottom of your rib cage.

- ➢ Pull your belly into your spine, and begin to twist slowly to your right, then come back to the center and go to the left side.
- ➢ Do this 10 times, rest, and repeat for a total of three sets.
- ➢ (If you want to make this more challenging, you can hold a weight. Just make sure to have a slight bend in your elbows while doing it, to take the pressure off your shoulders. Or you can lift your feet off the floor while doing the twist. Be sure your legs and feet stay stable, keeping them as still as possible.)

- ✶ **Hip Lift with Lower Leg Pull In: Balance Enough**

This exercise strengthens the hips, butt, and abdominals. These specific body parts are connected to holding yourself back because you don't feel enough, and not being able to balance work and play; they are the seat of your power. Strengthening this area will help you move forward in life and get unstuck.

This exercise stimulates the abdominal area specifically connected to the Sacral Chakra, which allows you to connect to your creativity, so you can find more play and can birth new ideas. Also, working one side and then the other brings balance to your masculine and feminine.

- Lie on your back on the floor
- Cross your right ankle over your left knee, and begin to lift your hips up off the floor, creating a bridge. Hold this for one minute, and then lower back down to your starting position.
- Then, keeping your legs in this position, bring your left knee in towards your belly, holding on around the left thigh. Hold this stretch for one minute.
- Repeat this two more times on the same side, and then do this same pattern of movements on the other side.
- (If you need to modify this, place both feet on the ground. Be sure to have your hips and knees lined up. Lift and lower your butt then bring in one leg toward your chest and back to the floor, repeating on the other side.)

★ Prone Snow Angel: Stream Enough

This exercise brings mobility and strength to the upper back. This part of your body includes the heart area. When you don't feel enough, you are guarding your heart, which inhibits you from fully giving and receiving. By working this area, you open up to giving and receiving and trusting yourself, others, and the Universe.

- Lie on the floor on your stomach.

- Tuck your chin, so you keep your neck in alignment with your spine.
- Your legs are straight and together as your belly draws in toward your spine.
- Your arms are at your sides with your palms facing down.
- Lift your arms off the floor and slowly bring them out away from your body and up over your head.
- Make sure to keep your shoulders down as your arms come up.
- Repeat for three sets of ten.
- (If you need to modify because you lack range of motion in your shoulders, bend your elbows slightly as your arms come up over your head. If you want to intensify this, you can also lift your legs off the floor when you lift your arms off the floor; as your arms go over your head, your legs open out, and they come back together as your arms come down.)

✶ Superman: Support Enough

This exercise strengthens the back, especially the lower back. The lower back area is about feeling supported. When you suffer with not-enough, you often have fear there will never be enough. This shows up in your life with money, material goods, and love. I find that even people who have a lot of money in the bank can still carry this deep-seated fear of not having enough.

- Lie face down on the floor.
- Keeping your legs together and your arms by your side, lift your upper body off the floor and then lower back down to the floor. This is a very small motion.
- Repeat for three sets of ten.
- (If you need to modify because you can't lie on the floor, you can do this lying on a bed. If you would like to make it more challenging, you can take your hands out to the side or you can hold a light weight.)

Exercises

It helps to begin movement by setting an intention. Energy follows intention. The answers you seek will come once you set your intention.

Once you set your intention, be aware throughout your day. Take it to another level, and set your intention to move your physical body to stir up that dormant energy. Your body is ready to liberate this, as it does not serve it.

During your movement or right after it would be ideal to be aware of what comes up. Is it thoughts? Visions? Everything is a piece of this puzzle of truth.

Then call your higher self to help you. Ask your higher self to guide you and show you clarity with what this hole is and how to begin to fill it.

Strength-building exercises:

- **The Exercise Movement Conducted with Mary.**

This specific movement builds strength.

- Stretch for your lower back begins with lying on the floor on your back, both knees bent, with feet on the floor.
- Take the right ankle and lay it on the left bent knee.
- Gently bring your left leg in toward your chest, and hold it there for at least thirty seconds.
- Repeat for the other side.
- Then conduct the movement called Superman. Begin lying on the floor on your stomach.
- Have your arms extended over your head and legs extended straight down, just like you are flying—like Superman!
- Begin to lift and lower just your upper body off the floor twenty times.
- Rest for fifteen seconds and repeat the exercise.

Chapter 7

Eating to Enough

BELIEVE IT OR NOT, food is a huge part of the not-enough syndrome. We use it to fill our emptiness, or we use it by cutting it out completely, starving our bodies because we don't feel enough. It's not the food that is the culprit: the not-enough syndrome is fueling what we do and how we interact with food.

When I was a teenager, the feelings of not-enough were at their all-time high. I would starve myself until the hunger forced me to eat, and then I would binge on items that would be instantly purged from my system, like grapes.

Without even consciously knowing it, I was trying to starve out or kill a feeling I didn't have words to express.

Now I know a sign for me to look deeper within is when I begin to do or not do something with food. Instead of depriving myself, now I take a step back, give my body the proper nutrients it needs, and begin the investigation into where I believe I'm not enough in my life.

Hippocrates said, "Let food be thy medicine and medicine be thy food." I firmly believe this is true. My journey began with personal training, and I came to realize that food was the next step in supporting overall wellness.

Most of us eat the standard American diet (SAD), which is loaded with sugar, chemicals, additives, and preservatives. This way of eating, causes the body to misfire. This misfire can show up in your nervous system and immune system, and it will perpetuate the not-enough syndrome.

Fresh, whole foods grown from the earth have a high vibration and contain the vitamins and minerals the body needs to thrive. The food that grows from the earth without processing is very easy for your body to assimilate.

Food is your fuel, so it's important to feed your physical body high-octane fuel for the performance of a lifetime.

This guide is based on years of experience and training in action. A simple rule to keep in mind is the more the degree of separation from the ground and your body, the more a food will make you feel separate and unfulfilled.

Eating foods that grow from the earth and go straight to your mouth is the best thing you can do to feel enough.

Chapter 8

Meal Guide to Enough:

Bio-individuality

"There's no one-size-fits-all diet. Each person is a unique individual with a highly individualized nutrition."

—IIN Joshua Rosenthal

THIS COMPLEX YET SIMPLE concept pertains to everyone who is ready to honor their uniqueness.

One person's food is another person's poison. There is no one-size-fits-all, although there are guidelines that will allow your body to feel its worth. Maybe the diet you are on is not working. Or maybe you feel terrible and know this is a signal that something needs to change.

Men and women eat differently, just as children eat differently than adults. People who work sitting at a computer daily eat differently than people who do heavy labor. If you think about it, you have eaten differently during different stages of your life.

There are many factors that shape bio-individuality, including:

1. Ancestry
2. Blood type
3. Metabolism
4. Personal tastes and preferences
5. Profession

My goal is to teach you to tune into your body and begin to listen to the messages it sends.

This will not happen overnight, but I can promise you the more you practice, the quicker you will "get" it.

You will develop and understand what types of food your body needs, when, and how much. You will no longer fill the emptiness or not-enough and instead just simply listen to what your body needs to thrive. You will move from allowing not-enough to send you signals to allowing your body to take over and send you signals of what it actually needs.

You will begin to discover what foods fuel you the best and then, before you know it, you will reach your health goals with fewer struggles. Trust your body, because it is highly intelligent. Your heart never forgets to beat, your lungs always breathe in and breathe out. This is validation that the body will tell you what food it needs to thrive and to feel good and balanced.

Follow bio-individuality using the *5 Core Pillars Food Guide* to get to enough that will last a lifetime.

Optimal health will create a world of lasting wellness and a feeling of enough. That is what we are trying to do, after all, isn't it?

Easy Summary of Eating to Enough: Include A Pillars Each Day.

❖ Pillar #1 – Water:

Drink half your body weight in ounces daily

❖ Pillar #2 - Greens

Examples of greens include: kale, collard greens, bok choy, Napa cabbage, mustard greens, arugula, endive

❖ Pillar #3 - Protein

Examples of protein include: chicken, turkey, lamb, beans, organic non-GMO tofu, chickpeas, hemp, nutritional yeast

- ❖ Pillar #4 - Carbs/Grains

Examples of grains include: quinoa, old fashioned Oats, millet, amaranth, buckwheat, and kasha, farro, steel-cut oats

- ❖ Pillar #5 - Fats

Examples of fats include: unrefined coconut oil, avocados, olive oil, raw cashews, walnuts, almonds, sesame seeds, hemp seeds, cold-water fatty fish like salmon, mackerel, and tuna, preferably wild-caught.

1st Core Pillar = Wonderful Water

Water: the first place to start!

Humans have no capacity to store "spare" water. We must quickly replace any that is lost. We are made up of sixty-percent water.

The typical pattern for many Americans is to have a few cups of coffee in the morning, more coffee mid-morning, a caffeinated beverage like iced tea at lunch, and then maybe a glass of wine or beer with dinner. Alcohol and caffeine are both diuretics, so many people are dehydrated and don't even realize it.

Water is vital for the body for so many reasons:

- ✓ Water is a highway that moves nutrients and waste between cells and organs.

- ✓ Nearly all chemical reactions of our metabolism involve water.
- ✓ Water is an essential component of the body's mechanisms to maintain proper PH balance. This leads to a healthier gut, which links directly to a healthy immune system.
- ✓ It is the major component of all the body fluids, like those that perform shock absorption, lubrication, and cleansing.
- ✓ Supports weight loss, because it replaces high-calorie drinks like soda and juices.
- ✓ Suppresses appetite. (Often, when we think we are hungry, our body is really just thirsty.)
- ✓ Supports healthy skin (helps flush out toxins and waste).
- ✓ Helps our body digest food properly.

Did you ever drink a big glass of water and feel full? Water is a great start to filling yourself with purity, when grappling with not enough. It will fill the emptiness and allow your body to flush out toxins.

This is the first place I begin with my clients, no matter what their goals are. Many of them report going to the bathroom more regularly, too, which helps them look and feel less bloated.

How much water is enough?

There is no one-sentence answer to this question. Every person needs a different amount, depending on their size, body composition, and activity level, as well as the temperature and humidity of the environment.

A simple method is this: drink half your body weight in ounces daily. For example, if you weigh 120 pounds, then your goal would be to drink sixty ounces of pure water daily.

3 Quick Tips to make water a HABIT

1. Set a reminder: set an alarm to go off on your phone, computer, or watch every hour; when it beeps, drink water.
2. Drink an eight-ounce glass of water:
   - ✓ Upon waking in the morning
   - ✓ Mid-morning
   - ✓ Before you eat your lunch
   - ✓ Mid-afternoon
   - ✓ Before you eat dinner
   - ✓ Before bed
3. Keep a log: track your intake of water throughout the day. This will increase your awareness around water and ensure you are staying on track with the correct intake for your body.

Once you begin to increase your intake, you will probably begin to feel it's boring and you are tired of drinking plain water. Here is the solution to this:

Sex it Up!:

1. Try hot or warm water with fresh lemon (very detoxifying). Bonus: lemon is recommended for opening the heart and increasing self-love in many essential oil companies (though I suggest fresh lemon over oil any day).

2. To cool water, add in the following, either separate or throw it all together:

- ✓ Fresh mint
- ✓ Fresh orange slices
- ✓ Fresh cucumber slices
- ✓ Fresh lemon or lime slices
- ✓ Fresh grapefruit slices
- ✓ Fresh strawberries or blueberries
- ✓ Anything fresh! Be creative to add sex appeal to your water! If you want to activate a specific chakra, put that colored food in your water.

3. Choose a fun glass or container that you enjoy drinking out of. One of my clients loved to drink out of a big, clear goblet, because it reminded her of the royal chalice and made her feel like a queen.

2nd Core Pillar = Good Greens

Greens are vital for the body in the many ways I describe throughout this chapter. A few key reasons it is important to eat greens daily:

- ✓ Promotes weight loss due to the high fiber content and antioxidants.
- ✓ Kale is high in calcium.
- ✓ Dark leafy greens help to purify your blood.
- ✓ U.S. Department of Agriculture recommends that adults consume at least three cups of dark greens veggies each week.
- ✓ There are no studies that state you can overdose on green leafy veggies. With this great news, I suggest eating a little of them at each meal, to make this a habit that sticks FOREVER!

Three times a day is easy. You don't have to make huge changes to your eating habits to include greens. Here is an example on how to get them in with every meal:

Breakfast: They go great with eggs

Lunch: They are yummy mixed in with a salad

Dinner: Eat as a side dish cooked with garlic

The Internet also offers an array of recipes that include dark, leafy greens.

3rd Core Pillar = Powerful Protein

Protein is a component of food made up of amino acids. Amino acids are the building blocks for major parts of a lean human body. They are crucial to the minute-by-minute regulation and maintenance of the body. Your body makes its own supply of amino acids, and you also must get some from food. Protein comes in many different forms.

Importance: Protein is the basic building block of cells and tissues that are needed to keep us strong. It is crucial for vital functions, regulation and maintenance of our bodies.

Trends: The current American diet trends encourage an increase in protein consumption (and carbohydrate reduction). There is another belief system that we do not need a lot of protein; it encourages people to eat much less protein. There is a very judgmental attitude in the field of nutrition, i.e., "my way is the only way." However, there must be a way that is not dogmatic. Try experimenting and see what works for you, your body, and your lifestyle.

Too little protein: Common symptoms include sugar and sweet cravings, feeling spacey and jittery, fatigue, weight loss, loss of healthy color in facial area, feeling weak, anemia, change in hair color and texture, skin inflammation (in severe cases), and pot belly (in severe cases).

Too much protein: Common symptoms include low energy, constipation, dehydration, lethargy, heavy feeling, weight gain, sweet cravings, feeling "tight" or stiff joints, body becomes overly acidic, kidney function declines (stress required to process excess proteins—the kidney faces increased pressure to filter toxins and waste), foul body odor, halitosis, and calcium loss to compensate for acidic status in body.

Things to consider: Your mind may disagree with what your body wants. Trust your body. It is rare for Americans in this day and age to be protein-deficient. Consider your heritage, ancestry, blood type, activity level, and life goals when choosing protein quantities. Protein consumption is a very personal thing—everyone needs a different amount.

4th Core Pillar = Great Carbs and Grains

Carbohydrate: what a dirty word!

My teacher, Joshua Rosenthal, at the Institute of Integrative Nutrition, said the following, which changed the way I viewed carbohydrates. I began to share this information with all of my clients, and they found it to be extremely helpful. As a society, we have been trained to be afraid of carbohydrates.

"The problem is people are not eating the types of carbohydrates nature intended." – Joshua Rosenthal

"The anti-carb movement should really be an anti-simple-carb movement." – Joshua Rosenthal

Let's just imagine for a moment that you never eat bread or pasta or any other "processed" carb again, and you only eat grains. The grains are what nature intended, and they bring satiation to your body.

Some great grains include:

- ✓ Quinoa
- ✓ Old-fashioned Oats
- ✓ Millet
- ✓ Amaranth
- ✓ Buckwheat
- ✓ Kasha

These are vital for your body because:

- ✓ The body absorbs them slowly, which provides long-lasting energy.
- ✓ High levels of dietary fiber (research supports a role of dietary fiber in reducing hunger and promoting satiety) and B vitamins
- ✓ Keeps the gastrointestinal tract healthy
- ✓ May reduce the risk of heart disease and cancer

- ✓ A natural way to feel full when you feel emptiness from not-enough

How much does the body need daily? The recommended daily allowance (RDA) of carbohydrates for people ages one year and older is 130 grams per day.

What exactly does this mean for you? There is no magic number for how much you should take in. Just know that your body needs carbs daily. Maybe you need more than your friend Sally. Whatever the case, play the trial-and-error game to find out what is perfect for your body.

I believe you need to get curious about the way your body handles carbohydrates. Everyone will be very different, so follow a *bio-individual prescription* with carbs/grains. This will be the key to your personal, long-lasting success. Please take into consideration your heritage, blood type, and what you do on a daily basis. Make note of how you feel daily: more energy, less energy, bloated, happier, depressed—these will be great signs that will help you know if you have the correct amount for your body.

5th Core Pillar = Fabulous Fats

Fats are vital for the body for many reasons. Here are a few key points:

1. Nourish the body's heart, brain, nerves, hormones, and every cell!
2. Good for the health of your hair, skin, and nails
3. Help the body feel full, so you eat less

Focus on eating *GOOD* fats daily to help lose weight, increase your energy, boost your immune system, and optimize your digestion.

Unrefined coconut oil is a good saturated fat source. This can aid in weight loss, because the body converts it quickly to energy. It also contains lauric acid, which is a medium-chain fatty acid found in only one naturally occurring place—human breast milk.

This is my take on it: if it is found in breast milk and that is the foundation of our nurturing and survival, it would be important for us to consume, since the body will innately remember it.

Coconut oil can withstand high heats, which makes it a great choice for cooking. When cooking at high heats, such as in the wok making stir fry, use coconut oil, since it can withstand the temperature without destroying its good health properties.

Other natural sources of good fats to include daily:

✓ Avocados

- ✓ Unrefined olive oil
- ✓ Raw nuts
- ✓ Sesame seeds
- ✓ Hemp seeds
- ✓ Cold-water fatty fish, like salmon, mackerel, and tuna

Be aware that some fats are refined and some are unrefined. Unrefined oils have the highest nutrient content and fullest flavor.

How much does the body need? The dietary guidelines for Americans (2005) recommend a maximum fat intake of twenty to thirty-five percent of total calories, with most of it coming from sources of polyunsaturated and monounsaturated fatty acids, like fish, nuts, and vegetable oils.

Here is the best guidance I can share so you don't pull your hair out trying to calculate this.

Avoid saturated fats, like cheese, milk, butters, and fatty meats ninety percent of the time. Only eat these about ten percent of the time, maybe even once a week.

NEVER eat trans fats, like in fast food and pre-packaged foods, including frozen dinners. I don't care how busy your schedule may be or how hungry you get... Avoid fast food at all costs. It takes just as much time to stop and buy a banana and some almond butter to hold you over until you can get more food. Fast food has a direct link to your mood and your mind.

Now that you understand the five core pillars of Eating to Enough, you can begin to use it. You want to make sure to eat *all of the core pillars daily* for optimum results. If you feel overwhelmed in getting started, I suggest you begin with water and then add on one thing every few days until they are all incorporated.

Resources

Basic Chakra System

Crown - 7th Chakra PURPLE: I AM ONE WITH THE DIVINE AND HONORING THAT WHICH IS WITHIN ME

Divine knowledge/wisdom – This chakra is fueled mostly by your breath, as it is mainly etheric in nature.

Eating foods that are naturally purple-colored will support this chakra, too.

Central location: At the top of your head.

Third eye - 6th Chakra INDIGO: I AM SEEING THE DIVINITY IN EVERYTHING.

Eating foods that are naturally indigo-colored will support this chakra, too.

Eyes, forehead, back of the head area, pineal.

Central location: In the center between your eyebrows.

Throat - 5th Chakra BLUE: I AM EXPRESSING DIVINE TRUTH.

This is connected to self-expression and life purpose. Eating fruit feeds this chakra. Eating foods that are naturally blue-colored will support this chakra, too.

Throat, neck, shoulders, ears, thyroid.

Central location: The neck and throat

Heart - 4th Chakra GREEN: I AM LOVE, I GIVE LOVE, AND I AM OPEN TO RECEIVING LOVE.

This is connected to love and connections. Eating all vegetables will feed this chakra. Eating foods that are naturally green-colored will support this chakra, too.

Circulatory system, upper back, chest, arms, and hands.

Central location: The chest between your breasts.

Solar Plexus - 3rd Chakra YELLOW: I AM CENTERED IN MY PASSION & PURPOSE.

Digestive system, upper abdominal area, mid-back area. This is connected to your Divine will power and identity. Eating grains and vegetables that grow over three-feet tall will feed this chakra. Eating foods that are naturally yellow-colored will support this chakra, too.

Central location: At your solar plexus, which is between the belly button and bottom of rib cage

Sacral - 2nd Chakra ORANGE: I AM CONFIDENTLY CREATIVE

Lymphatic system, reproductive system, including breasts, urinary system, blood, lower abdominal area, and lower back

Central location: The lower abdominal area below your naval.

This is connected to your emotions and desires. Eating vegetables that grow up to three-feet high and drinking water will feed this chakra. Eating foods that are naturally orange-colored will support this chakra, too.

Root - 1st Chakra RED: I AM SAFE AND SECURE

Bones (skeleton), nails, teeth, hair, rectum, colon, legs, and feet.

This is connected to your physical existence. Eating protein and root vegetables feeds this chakra. Eating foods that are naturally red-colored will support this chakra, too.

Central location: The base of your spine

Case Studies

Libbie

Prior to using the program, Libbie described her consumption of food as, "I just shoved it in and hurried on to the next thing." She also believed she wouldn't be impacted by the program, because of, in her own words, "having done a lot of self-work over the past years."

She never felt she was worthy of slowing down and enjoying her food and creating health via her food. Libbie knew she "should" eat healthy, but the knowing and not doing was just another way she used to prove to herself she was not enough.

After a couple of days, using the easy-to-follow plan and exercise, she had some profound shifts:

- ★ She understood that her feelings of not-enoughness stemmed from her relationship with her father.

- ✶ She noticed she was more sensory, enjoyed the experience of eating, and began to savor her food.
- ✶ She began to enjoy taking care of herself and using food as a support

Danielle

For years, she had been using food and diets to deprive and punish herself, believing she was unworthy. She also felt disconnected from her higher self.

After completing the program, she:

- ✶ Automatically began to say, "I'm worthy" before a meal.
- ✶ Knows she is worthy of taking the best care of herself and is doing it
- ✶ In her words, "doesn't need to take anything away from myself."

Stacey

Prior to utilizing the book, Stacey carried around not-enough all her life. She felt like she had to prove herself and beat herself up when she made mistakes. Her inner dialog prevented her from feeling joy and gratitude on a regular basis.

Stacey's entire framework has shifted. She now believes she is truly enough, and she believes this "will be a part of my lifelong toolkit."

By using the exercises, her consumption of red meat, alcohol, diary, and caffeine have plummeted, and she lost weight, too.

Gail

Gail used to numb herself through food and feel very disconnected from her life. By following the exercises and reading the stories of others, she says, "I much more aware of my thoughts before, during, and after eating."

Julie

Julie is the middle child of three. She spent her childhood yearning to have the connection her brother had with her father or the attention her younger sister received from her mother.

The reaction of this environment made her a goal-setter and achiever. When she received accolades, they felt hollow. For most of her life, she struggled with feelings of not measuring up and had low self-confidence. Her married life was not providing the love and partnership she craved, and the result was arguments.

Before utilizing the movement exercises, Julie was fifty pounds overweight and eating to feed the frustration and sadness. As she began to move toward enough, she felt her core strength, and it reminded her she was enough. She started to stand taller and felt her core essence being activated.

In her words, "My self-confidence took this tiny foothold and blossomed with healthy, forthright communication. Food choices came with ease and mindfulness of wanting to nourish me, because 'I am ENOUGH.' Looking in the mirror, I used to see a common girl with out-of-control crazy curls. Now, I see a depth of love in a gorgeous woman looking back at me, and those crazy curls are just a perfect part of the awesome woman I see. Because, from my very core with movements and their connections, I know '*I AM ENOUGH.*'

"Almost immediately, moving to the mantra 'I AM ENOUGH' took seed in my core. In just seven days, I felt stronger."

Merrie

She spent her life being a person who would drop everything, including her family, to help others. Merrie allowed people to take advantage of her kindness, always putting her own wants, needs, and desires last.

She would often not participate in community or get involved in activities because she was overcome with shame and not-enough. She was bullied and would often make excuses for others' behaviors. As a teenager, she was sexually accosted, and the police blamed her. She was experiencing all the symptoms of not-enough.

As she began the movement exercises, she loved knowing how all the movement correlated to her body and spirit. Having the knowledge that it wasn't just exercise strongly motivated her to be and do more for herself.

Merrie has begun to go out and participate in crafting with others. She is sleeping better and enjoying others' company, including enjoying her alone time. Her relationship with her husband has improved, allowing a new sense of intimacy, and she told him she loved him for the first time in years. She has begun to say no to situations that don't feel good to her or where she was being taken advantage of.

In her own words, "I told my cousin no, I would not take care of her responsibilities while she was out with co-workers. I started to feel bad but held firm on my decision. I spent the last year and a half giving up my days off and time with my family and sick dog to care for my aunt, while my cousin worked overtime or went out with friends. Well! If that's not transformation, I don't know what is.

"There has been a definite shift for me. I was very calm throughout my day now, even though there are the usual triggers. I truly am a different person, a person I love and whom allow others to love."

The Last Chapter of Enoughness

(At This Moment)

IN ONE MOMENT, you can change the entire trajectory of your life. It starts with awareness then a choice to make a change. I have given you the blueprint to create your future life of being, feeling, breathing, and living enough.

Do one thing every day, and you will begin to paint your life's canvas with enough. You will not only change your life but the lives of your children and the people around you. It is infectious to remember your worth.

Did you ever sit in a room listening to a powerhouse speaker? Could you feel their energy and compassion for change? That is exactly what it will be like when you use the blueprint given and start becoming the change you have dreamed of.

Follow the guidelines given, and before you know it, you will be experiencing life more fully. If you feel overwhelmed or confused, know that it is your not-enough syndrome rearing its head. Every time I feel confusion, I realize this is something false in my brain and a side effect of not feeling enough. So, step back for a moment, and break things down to smaller, bite-size chunks to make some kind of movement into your enoughness and get the process going.

As I have shared a glimpse into parts of my life to help you understand where I came from and how I moved through experiences, it is important for me to articulate how blessed I am for every experience that has been hard and hurtful.

I am very grateful for my parents, grandparents, family members, friends, and partners, who shaped who I am today. I love them very deeply and understand that, during my life's journey, they, too, were moving through their own life's discoveries.

They did the best they could with what they had at that time in their life. I understand this more now, as I reflect back during the creation of this book. Is there a way for you to reflect back and know that your life's experiences happened to help your soul evolution and growth? You can't stay prisoner or victim of circumstance when you are choosing to be enough.

When and if you have a moment where you feel alone or like you are falling back into old habits, or maybe even like you are at a different level of not-enough, come back to this book and use the blueprint again. It is like a muscle: the more you work on it, the stronger and more flexible it becomes.

You are not alone! There are many people struggling with remembering their enoughness.

When you need a quick re-set, remember this: God/Divine Intelligence created every particle of you, including your physical body, and this energy is your matrix, which means *you were born enough.*

Thank You

THANK YOU, Jennifer Urrezio, for believing in my vision, which was certainly just a conglomerate mess when we first started working together. You saw the greater message that I was to share with the world, and you kept me focused for over a year to make it come to life.

Thank you, Danielle Molella, for jumping in to create the magical cover. Your support was greatly needed during this journey.

Thank you, AJ Mihrzad and your 10x team, for consistent support. You have taught me that I am strong enough to play outside my comfort zone and grow deeply while making massive impact in the world. I appreciate you!

Thank you, Kathryn F. Galán with Wynnpix Productions, for editing and setting this up to be an easy publish. Without your drive and persistence, this may have sat in a Word document for years.

My dear husband Joe, you have always allowed me to take risks to fulfill my dreams. It is your belief in me, that I can do anything my heart desires, that keeps me going, even when things feel difficult.

My children have taught me the deeper workings of myself and how strong I really am. I am grateful to you both always.

Lots of gratitude I offer to my mom, dad, grandma, sister, and family members, for helping me become who I am today.

Thanks to all my friends who have supported me in reminding me I am enough in every moment.

Thank you to everyone who has purchased this book and taken the time to use the tools given to make real change in your life. We are all connected, so, as you grow and change, it helps others do the same.

Most importantly, I am very grateful for God. If I did not have Your presence in my life, supporting me to remember that You are within me and around me always, I may not have kept going in my journey.

About Ondrea Lynn

ONDREA LYNN'S PASSION is to help you know that you are enough. She mentors you into enoughness in all areas of your life: body, mind, spirit, and emotions. She has the ability to see your true nature through the eyes of the Divine and helps you embody and create that true Divine reflection in the world.

She began her own spiritual awakening as a teenager, when she became a metaphysical mentor and Archangel channel. She has extensive experience in body-mind wellness, is a graduate of the Institute of Integrated Nutrition, affiliated with the Teachers College at Columbia University. Some of her certifications include NASM fitness trainer, Reiki, Shamanism, Master Angel Practitioner, Chakra, Arcturian, and quantum healing.

Ondrea has helped thousands of people reach their personal health-and-wellness goals and improve their physical and nutritional health, as well as their emotional and spiritual wellbeing.

Her efforts in health and wellness have been featured in an article and on the cover of *Woman's World Magazine*. She appeared as a personal trainer on Lifetime television's *Mission Makeover,* season two.

Ondrea is highly intuitive and has integrated all of her certifications in health and wellness, as well as in multi-dimensional healing, to help you level up as a human by embracing your enoughness through all areas of Divine health. Not having Divine health means something in your consciousness doesn't believe you can attain this, so it is time to be in alignment with your birthright and allow all the higher guides of Light and Love, such as your Higher Self, Archangels, Ascended Masters, and Star Beings, to support you into remembering.

Thank you for taking the time to move through this book. I invite you to make this a tool to use often in your life. Be sure to write a review on Amazon and then send me an email, sharing what awareness came from reading this and all the healing that has come from it, too! Here is my email: ondrealynnbook@gmail.com.

I look forward to hearing from you!

www.ondrealynn.com

Find me on social media:

YouTube: https://www.youtube.com/channel/UC8bpeY6RCk2J4woEMmcRFEg?view_as=subscriber

Facebook: https://www.facebook.com/Ondrea-Lynn-282602009657/

Instagram: https://www.instagram.com/ondrealynn/?hl=en

Made in the USA
Middletown, DE
26 November 2020

25301265R00097